AMANDA WHITTINGTON

Amanda Whittington is one of the most performed playwrights in the UK. She has written more than forty original plays for theatre and audio drama, including *Be My Baby*, *The Thrill of Love*, *Kiss Me Quickstep*, *Mighty Atoms*, *Atalanta Forever*, *Amateur Girl*, *Ladies' Day*, *Ladies Down Under* and *Ladies Unleashed*. Amanda wrote the book for *Fisherman's Friends: The Musical*. Her extensive work for BBC Radio 4 includes the award-winning series *D for Dexter*, *The Nine Days Queen*, *The Dock Nuremberg* and *The Archers*. In 2017, she was awarded a PhD by Publication by Hudderfield University for her thesis *Bad Girls and Blonde Bombshells: Lived Feminisms in Popular Theatre*.

Other Titles in this Series

Mike Bartlett
THE 47TH
ALBION
BULL
GAME
AN INTERVENTION
KING CHARLES III
MIKE BARTLETT PLAYS: TWO
MRS DELGADO
SCANDALTOWN
SNOWFLAKE
VASSA *after* Gorky
WILD

Jez Butterworth
THE FERRYMAN
JERUSALEM
JEZ BUTTERWORTH PLAYS: ONE
JEZ BUTTERWORTH PLAYS: TWO
MOJO
THE NIGHT HERON
PARLOUR SONG
THE RIVER
THE WINTERLING

Caryl Churchill
BLUE HEART
CHURCHILL PLAYS: THREE
CHURCHILL PLAYS: FOUR
CHURCHILL PLAYS: FIVE
CHURCHILL: SHORTS
CLOUD NINE
DING DONG THE WICKED
A DREAM PLAY *after* Strindberg
DRUNK ENOUGH TO SAY I LOVE YOU?
ESCAPED ALONE
FAR AWAY
GLASS. KILL. BLUEBEARD'S FRIENDS.
    IMP.
HERE WE GO
HOTEL
ICECREAM
LIGHT SHINING IN BUCKINGHAMSHIRE
LOVE AND INFORMATION
MAD FOREST
A NUMBER
PIGS AND DOGS
SEVEN JEWISH CHILDREN
THE SKRIKER
THIS IS A CHAIR
THYESTES *after* Seneca
TRAPS
WHAT IF IF ONLY

Natasha Gordon
NINE NIGHT

Lucy Kirkwood
BEAUTY AND THE BEAST
    with Katie Mitchell
BLOODY WIMMIN
THE CHILDREN
CHIMERICA
HEDDA *after* Ibsen
IT FELT EMPTY WHEN THE HEART
    WENT AT FIRST BUT IT IS
    ALRIGHT NOW
LUCY KIRKWOOD PLAYS: ONE
MOSQUITOES
NSFW
RAPTURE
TINDERBOX
THE WELKIN

Liz Lochhead
BLOOD AND ICE
DRACULA *after* Stoker
EDUCATING AGNES ('The School
    for Wives') *after* Molière
GOOD THINGS
LIZ LOCHHEAD: FIVE PLAYS
MARY QUEEN OF SCOTS GOT
    HER HEAD CHOPPED OFF
MEDEA *after* Euripides
MISERYGUTS ('The Miser')
    & TARTUFFE *after* Molière
PERFECT DAYS
THEBANS *after* Euripides & Sophocles
THON MAN MOLIÈRE

Nat McCleary
THROWN

Rona Munro
THE ASTRONAUT'S CHAIR
BOLD GIRLS
CAPTAIN CORELLI'S MANDOLIN
    after Louis de Bernières
THE HOUSE OF BERNARDA ALBA
    after Lorca
THE INDIAN BOY
IRON
THE JAMES PLAYS
JAMES IV: QUEEN OF THE FIGHT
THE LAST WITCH
LITTLE EAGLES
LONG TIME DEAD
THE MAIDEN STONE
MARY
MARY BARTON *after* Gaskell
MARY SHELLEY'S FRANKENSTEIN
    after Mary Shelley
PANDAS
SCUTTLERS
STRAWBERRIES IN JANUARY
    from de la Chenelière
YOUR TURN TO CLEAN THE STAIR
    & FUGUE

Jessica Swale
BLUE STOCKINGS
THE JUNGLE BOOK *after* Kipling
NELL GWYNN

debbie tucker green
BORN BAD
DEBBIE TUCKER GREEN PLAYS: ONE
DIRTY BUTTERFLY
EAR FOR EYE
HANG
NUT
A PROFOUNDLY AFFECTIONATE,
    PASSIONATE DEVOTION TO
    SOMEONE (– *NOUN*)
RANDOM
STONING MARY
TRADE & GENERATIONS
TRUTH AND RECONCILIATION

Amanda Whittington
BE MY BABY
KISS ME QUICKSTEP
LADIES' DAY
LADIES DOWN UNDER
LADIES UNLEASHED
MIGHTY ATOMS
SATIN 'N' STEEL
THE THRILL OF LOVE

Amanda Whittington

THE
INVINCIBLES

NICK HERN BOOKS

London

www.nickhernbooks.co.uk

A Nick Hern Book

The Invincibles first published in Great Britain as a paperback original in 2023 by Nick Hern Books Limited, The Glasshouse, 49a Goldhawk Road, London W12 8QP

The Invincibles copyright © 2023 Amanda Whittington

Amanda Whittington has asserted her right to be identified as the author of this work

Cover design: design:**feast**creative.com

Designed and typeset by Nick Hern Books, London
Printed in the UK by Mimeo Ltd, Huntingdon, Cambridgeshire PE29 6XX

A CIP catalogue record for this book is available from the British Library

ISBN 978 1 83904 289 8

www.nickhernbooks.co.uk/environmental-policy

Introduction
Amanda Whittington

The Invincibles is the story of Sterling Ladies, the great Dagenham works' football team whose unbeaten record was unsurpassed in World War One. As I researched the untold story of the Dagenham Invincibles, the Lionesses were winning their famous victory in EURO 2022. Writing the play in 2023, I felt the pull of England's Women's World Cup.

The play opened in early September, meaning the tournament ran through our rehearsals. Could we weave a 2023 story into the 1917–18 world? It felt like a golden opportunity to harness the excitement of the World Cup and trace the invisible thread from the Munitionettes to the Lionesses. Two teams in one play? Game on!

Our first day of rehearsal coincided with England's scheduled Final 16 match. Yet, what if they fell at the Group Stage? We felt it was a risk worth taking. Led by James Grieve, our brilliant creative team and cast took a giant leap of faith in a story that was yet to be fully written. I'm so grateful to every one of them for trusting the process and believing not only in me but the Lionesses' will to win.

On August 7th, with three scenes sketched from the Group Stage wins, we all came together in the rehearsal room for an 8.30 a.m. kick-off. England beat Nigeria 4–2 on penalties and we celebrated the win with a read-through of the play in progress. The extraordinary story of Sterling Ladies was in place and we began to infuse it with the energy and drama of the Women's World Cup.

As we now know, England powered through to the final. As they did, the heroines of 1918 felt thrillingly alive in the room. Nell describes herself as 'a spark, a flame, a fire', and that's what we set out to explore and express: how it *feels* to play – and, as women through time have found, *not* to play – the game you love.

Like Sterling Ladies, the Lionesses didn't get their fairytale ending but hey, that's football – and theatre. On and off the pitch, there are battles still to fight and our story captures that, too. But this play was written and performed in celebration of a thrilling summer of women's football, a century of progress and an unbeaten, eternal Invincible spirit.

September 2023

The Invincibles was first performed at Queen's Theatre Hornchurch on 7 September 2023. The cast was as follows:

GLADYS	Gemma Barnett (she/her)
ADA	Georgia Bruce (they/them)
CHOLLY/ BRIAN BADEN	Simon Darwen (he/him)
MAYA	Yanexi Enriquez (she/her)
SAMMY/HANNAH	Emma Feeney (she/her)
TRIXIE	Rebecca Hayes (they/them)
MAUD	Nikita Johal (she/her)
NELL	Eleanor Kane (she/they)
JAMES/GUY	Steve Simmonds (he/him)

Director	James Grieve (he/him)
Designer	Laura Ann Price (she/they)
Lighting Designer	Martha Godfrey (they/them)
Sound Design & Composition	Holly Khan (she/her)
Movement Directior	Lucie Pankhurst (she/her)
Casting	Jenkins McShane (she/her)
Historical Consultant	Steve Bolton (he/him)
Assistant Director	Rebecca Goh (they/them)
Musical Director	Andrew Linham (he/him)
Accent Coach	Mary Howland (she/her)
Football Coach	Lily Jones (she/her)
QTH Creative Lead	Kate Lovell (she/her)
Executive Producer	Mathew Russell (he/him)

Characters

2023
MAYA LEWIS, *seventeen, female*
SAMMY LEWIS, *early forties, female*
IDA SHEPHERD, *pre-recorded* Grass in the Clouds *presenter,
    twenties, female*
SOPHIE JONES, *pre-recorded* Grass in the Clouds *presenter,
    twenties, female*

1917
SOLDIER, *male*
GLADYS FAIRMAN, *twenty-three, female*
ADA FAIRMAN, *twenty-six, female*
JAMES FAIRMAN, *early fifties, male*
HANNAH FAIRMAN, *forties, female*
NELL MARCHANT, *seventeen, female*
GUY BURNEY, *mid-fifties, male*
ED 'CHOLLY' CHOLERTON, *early thirties, male*
MAUD READER, *twenty-four, female*
TRIXIE PETERS, *twenty-two, female*
BRIAN BADEN, *mid-forties, male*

The Invincibles moves between the two seasons played by
Sterling Ladies from 1917–19 and the summer of the 2023 FIFA
Women's World Cup. The two worlds coexist in the same
space; the Fairman family home is the Lewis family home.

*This text went to press before the end of rehearsals and so may
differ slightly from the play as performed.*

ACT ONE

1.

MAYA LEWIS *stands immersed in an atmospheric soundscape of the 2023 Women's World Cup. From the chanting crowds and the news clips rises a football commentary.*

COMMENTARY (*voice-over*). The day has finally come: July 20th 2023, the FIFA Women's World Cup. With thirty-two teams over six confederations, record-breaking ticket sales and worldwide television coverage, it's the biggest and the best of all time. In all four corners of the globe – game on!

As the soundscape tracks back in time, snapshots of football commentary lead to the sound of gunfire on the Western Front. From the cacophony, a WORLD WAR ONE SOLDIER *recites a 'Letter from the Trenches' by J. B. Priestley, as if his own.*

SOLDIER. My dear parents, I am writing this in my dugout. Last night, our troops made an attack on the German front line. It was literally hell upon earth: the sickly smell of cordite, an incessant stream of bullets, the sky lit up with a mad medley of shells, searchlights, star lights. You would hardly recognise me if you saw me. I am a mask of mud.

As the company sing 'Keep the Home Fires Burning', NELL MARCHANT *appears. She stands shoulder-to-shoulder with* MAYA.

COMPANY.
They were summoned from the hillside
They were called in from the glen
And the country found them ready
At the stirring call for men
Let no tears add to their hardships
As the soldiers pass along

And although your heart is breaking
Make it sing this cheery song
Keep the home fires burning
While your hearts are yearning
Though your lads are far away
They dream of home
There's a silver lining
Through the dark cloud shining
Turn the dark clouds inside out
Till the boys come home
(Till the girls)
Till the boys come home
(Till the girls)
Till the boys
(It's coming)
Come
(It's coming)
Home.

2.

Maya's home. 108 Park Lane, Hornchurch. Saturday July 22nd, 2023.

Morning. MAYA *wears an England football top. She has airpods in and watches England vs Haiti on her iPhone. She holds her feelings within but there's an intensity to her gaze. We hear the commentary she's listening to.*

COMMENTARY (*voice-over*). And when it comes to World Cup penalties, England have failed with their last three. But here's Georgia Stanway, she's scored all seven of her attempts for England.

SAMMY, MAYA*'s mother, comes home, dressed for work.*

SAMMY. Maya?

COMMENTARY (*voice-over*). Can she do it again?

SAMMY. 'Good morning, Ma.'

COMMENTARY (*voice-over*). Oh, a magnificent save from Kerly Théus! World-class!

SAMMY. Maya!

MAYA *pulls out her earbuds and shields her phone.*

MAYA. What y'doing 'ere?

SAMMY. What are you? Still in your PJs.

MAYA. I'm not.

SAMMY. At eleven in the morning.

MAYA. You're meant to be at work.

SAMMY. I am at work. I got a valuation. Claire phoned in sick, so I'm…

MAYA. Why don't you go to it, then?

SAMMY. Park Lane, innit? Three doors down. An' I 'ope to God I don't get it.

MAYA. Why?

SAMMY. Agent, vendor, stone's throw? No, thank you very much.

MAYA (*shrugs*). Don't go.

SAMMY. Ain't how the world works, Maya. Ain't how the world works.

SAMMY *checks her look in the mirror.* MAYA *puts her airpods in.*

COMMENTARY (*voice-over*). Now just a minute – they're checking the goalkeeper's position when Stanway struck the ball…

SAMMY. You get up, get dressed an' get on with it.

COMMENTARY (*voice-over*). Was Kerly Théus off her line? She was!

SAMMY. Work 'ard, play 'ard.

COMMENTARY (*voice-over*). Georgia Stanway with a second chance from the penalty spot…

MAYA. Yes!

COMMENTARY (*voice-over*). The Lionesses are go!

SAMMY. Maya? (*Fixes* MAYA *with a look.*) So, tomorrow?

MAYA. What?

MAYA *takes out her earbuds.*

SAMMY. Tomorrow. We're going up London.

MAYA. Since when?

SAMMY. We'll do a bit of shopping, see a few sights; have a Drag Show Brunch on the South Bank.

MAYA. I don't think so.

SAMMY. Why not? Be a laugh. Do you good. Do us both good, a trip out together. Mother an' daughter. Be nice.

MAYA. Why would I go to a drag show wi' you?

SAMMY. West End, then? They do Sundays now. *Harry Potter*, *Back to the Future*, *Tina: The Musical*, God rest 'er soul.

MAYA. Take Nan.

SAMMY. I wanna take you.

MAYA. I said no.

SAMMY. Fine. No problem. Just thought I'd check. Cos, me, I'd 'ave jumped at a chance like this at your age.

MAYA. You was never my age.

SAMMY. I'd a bin out there painting the town.

MAYA. I got plans.

SAMMY. What plans?

MAYA. My plans.

SAMMY. Good, do they possibly feature fresh air an' exercise?

MAYA. I ain't a dog.

SAMMY. Y'could try a little run? Pick up me prescription, it's ready.

MAYA. Can't you?

SAMMY. Gaw'on, please. Before two. If that fits with your 'ectic schedule of doing naff-all for the last five weeks.

MAYA. It's the 'olidays.

SAMMY. It's actually not when you're not going back.

MAYA. I'm still busy, aren't I? Planning me future.

SAMMY. You're seventeen, Maya.

MAYA. So when me results come, I'm ready.

SAMMY. This is a golden time between school and whatever comes next. No ties, no responsibilities –

MAYA. No one telling us what to do, where to go, who to be?

SAMMY. Don't waste it, that's all I'm saying. Don't be sat here messing around with your phone –

MAYA. Don't get pissed on prosecco with RuPaul.

SAMMY. I'm trying to 'ave a serious –

MAYA. Go to Pret. 'Ave a sandwich. Smashed avo.

SAMMY. We could go Lakeside, 'ave one together.

MAYA. You're going up London.

SAMMY. Don't have to.

MAYA. You want to.

SAMMY. But if you wanna do something? Get out the 'ouse an' away from it all.

MAYA. I ain't watching.

SAMMY. No?

Beat.

MAYA. No.

SAMMY. Cos we ain't going back down that road.

MAYA. We won't.

SAMMY. This time last year, the Euros on telly an' you –

MAYA. I'm over all that.

SAMMY. What's done is done.

MAYA. Yep.

> MAYA *looks* SAMMY *in the eye.*

SAMMY. Good. Cos y'know there's a big wide world out there waiting –

MAYA. It's eleven. You're late.

SAMMY. We don't want these four walls closing in on ya.

MAYA. They won't.

SAMMY. Again.

MAYA. They won't.

> *Beat.*

SAMMY. Done your physio?

MAYA. Not yet.

SAMMY. It's important.

MAYA. I know.

> *Beat.*

SAMMY. Only a game, innit, ey?

MAYA. Go.

SAMMY. Maya –

MAYA. S'only a game.

> MAYA *offers a smile.* SAMMY *returns it with an awkward hug. Leaves with difficulty.*

MAYA *listens. Waits until she's gone. Feels the silence. Puts airbuds in and returns to the match.*

COMMENTARY (*voice-over*). Half-time whistle here in Brisbane. There's little between the two sides but a contested penalty leaves us England one – Haiti nil.

3.

Fairman home. 108 Park Lane, Hornchurch. A Saturday in July, 1917. ADA FAIRMAN *works on an upturned Raleigh Ladies' Roadster bicycle. She's fully absorbed in the routine tasks: tightening nuts and bolts, oiling the chain, checking tyres.* ADA *sings to herself as she works.*

ADA.
  Keep the home fires burning
  While your hearts are yearning
  Though your lads are far away
  They dream of home
  There's a silver lining
  Through the dark cloud shining
  Turn the dark clouds inside out
  Till the boys come home –

  GLADYS, *her sister, breezes in.*

GLADYS. Sun's out, bed's made an' you'll be in trouble.

ADA. Says who?

GLADYS. Still in your overalls, grease on your 'ands.

ADA. Sat'day morning, it's what y'do.

GLADYS. What *you* do.

ADA. Repairs an' maintenance.

GLADYS. Don't you wanna make her feel welcome?

ADA. Who?

GLADYS. The new 'ousecat.

ADA. Miaow.

GLADYS. The Girl.

ADA. She'll take us as she finds us, Ma says.

GLADYS. In me best bib an' tucker. Well?

    ADA *gives* GLADYS *a cursory glance.*

ADA. Lipstick?

GLADYS. A little.

ADA. She's from London.

GLADYS. Quite.

ADA. Not West End, East End. Shoreditch, Stepney, Bow.

GLADYS. Why d'you say it like that? (*Sinister.*) 'Bow'.

ADA (*sings*).
   'I do not know'
   Say the great bells –

GLADYS. They ain't all poor, sick an' afflicted.

ADA. Diseased an' 'alf-starving in 'ovels.

GLADYS. She's a Munitionette.

ADA. An' y'know what they're up to in Romford.

GLADYS. She's coming for work. War work.

ADA. Away from 'ome with the money to do what they like.

GLADYS. Not in 'ornchurch an' not at the Sterling. It's clean work, she's doing. No cordite, phosphorus, gunpowder –

ADA. Bug powder. Y'got it?

GLADYS. Don't need it.

ADA. No? She's in your bed.

GLADYS. She's a paying guest, Ada. In our Ernest's room.

ADA. Father won't 'ave it.

GLADYS. Ma told 'im, she said if it 'elp with the 'ousehold budget –

ADA. An't you 'eard? They 'ad a right set-to. Pa says we're keepin' the room as 'e left it, Ma says three grown gals can't share. So as the eldest –

GLADYS. You're not.

ADA. As the eldest still living at 'ome, I said I'd move over an' not touch 'is things.

GLADYS. An' I 'ave to sleep wi' a stranger?

ADA. She won't be for long.

GLADYS. Ada!

ADA (*sings*).
    'Ere comes a candle to light you to bed,
    'Ere comes a chopper to chop off –

GLADYS. Y'know Ma said treat 'er like a sister? Don't!

    JAMES FAIRMAN, *their father, comes home with a bag of allotment vegetables.*

JAMES. Oi!

GLADYS. Father…

JAMES. They can 'ear yer 'in Dagenham. Shrieking.

ADA. It's Gladys.

GLADYS. It's 'er.

JAMES (*to* GLADYS). An' what's that on yer face?

GLADYS. Royal Vinola to give us a bloom.

JAMES. On yer mouth. Wipe it off.

ADA. Wash it out.

As ADA *throws* GLADYS *a rag,* JAMES *throws* GLADYS *a look.*

JAMES. An' you can sort this lot. (*Dumps the bag.*) Carrots, spuds, beans from the allotment.

GLADYS. Bin a good growin' season.

JAMES. Needs to be.

GLADYS. Wi' the shortages.

JAMES. An' the government farming out girls so they don't 'ave to feed 'em.

GLADYS. I'm not sure that's quite why she's coming.

ADA. She'll eat like a horse.

GLADYS. You eat like a donkey.

ADA. You look like a donkey.

JAMES. Post come, 'as it?

GLADYS (*to* ADA). 'As it?

ADA. On the side. There's four or five but –

JAMES. From Ernest?

ADA. Be still at the sorting office, I bet.

GLADYS. They'll have a backlog with all that's…

JAMES. Postwoman. She only lifts 'alf a bag.

GLADYS. But no news is good news.

ADA. An' it is good news. *Daily Mirror* says with the Sopwith Camels, the Yanks going in…

JAMES *goes to leave.*

GLADYS. There will be a letter, Father. He'll be home before you can say –

In comes HANNAH FAIRMAN, *their mother, ushering in their new lodger,* NELL MARCHANT.

HANNAH. Don't be shy, gal. You're 'ere now.

NELL *wears a ragged coat and a pained expression.*

You're 'ere, so let's be 'aving that winter coat off in July.

HANNAH *tries to take* NELL*'s coat but she wraps it around herself.* ADA *raises her eyebrows to* GLADYS. HANNAH *sees the look.*

Miss Eleanor Marchant. Here as part of the voluntary billeting of civilians to Chelmsford and District on work of national importance.

Known to her friends as Nell, I believe?

NELL *doesn't respond.* HANNAH *soldiers on.*

This is Mr Fairman.

JAMES *gives* NELL *a cursory nod.*

Our eldest gal, she's married now but this is our daughter Gladys.

ADA. The spinster.

GLADYS. Pot–kettle.

HANNAH. Her sister, Ada.

ADA. Short for Adelaide.

As ADA *introduces herself,* TRIXIE PETERS *bowls in.*

TRIXIE. Since when?

GLADYS. Ssshush!

TRIXIE. Sorry!

ADA (*nods to* TRIXIE). Trixie Peters, our sister-to-be.

TRIXIE (*to* NELL). I live three doors down.

HANNAH. On Park Lane, Nell.

TRIXIE. Thought I'd just drop by, say 'ow do.

HANNAH. Remember that: 108 Park Lane.

JAMES. You forgot the boy?

   Beat.

HANNAH. How could I?

JAMES. Our son.

HANNAH. Our youngest.

GLADYS. Our brother.

ADA. Our pal's betrothed.

TRIXIE. Ernest.

JAMES. Gunner, Royal Field Artillery.

GLADYS. Do you have brothers and sisters, Nell?

ADA. A brother? A sister?

HANNAH. Well, y'ave now.

JAMES. It's board an' lodgings, woman. That's all.

HANNAH. An' come Monday, she's part of the Sterling family. (*Fixes* JAMES *with a look.*) Tell 'er, Father. Tell 'er all about it.

JAMES. Sterling Telephone and Electrical Company. Rainham Road, Dagenham. Manufacturer of wireless equipment: crystal receivers, radio head-telephones, loudspeakers. Parts sourced from Ericsson but, latterly, making our own.

HANNAH. Girls? Tell us what *you* do up there?

GLADYS. I'm in the Machine Room.

ADA. Assembly Room.

TRIXIE. Me too.

ADA. Wherever you go, you'll find a good gang of gals.

GLADYS. It's physical work –

TRIXIE. Twelve hours a day –

ADA. But we're doing our bit –

GLADYS. An' all told, it's the best situation in Essex.

JAMES. So keep your nose clean. We've a name to uphold.

ADA. We ain't adopting 'er, are we?

JAMES. A good name with a family firm, so you keep an eye.
    It's your brother's future when he's home.

TRIXIE. An' a married man, ey?

ADA. Might be our future too?

NELL. Ain't Kynoch?

HANNAH. Beg your pardon?

NELL. Ain't Kynoch Works? Where they send all the scrubbers.

    ADA *and* TRIXIE *stifle a laugh.*

HANNAH. Now, we don't talk like that –

NELL. They do, they ship 'em out there 'stead of 'olloway.

HANNAH. Rumour an' 'earsay.

NELL. Making shells what blow up in your 'ands. Acetone.
    I know a gal says her best sister were drenched in it, set
    alight in 'er bed. Cos you're sleeping in sheds wi' 'em all
    like the workhouse, the asylum.

GLADYS. Kynochtown, it were built for the workers at Shell
    'aven Creek.

ADA. On the bogland.

NELL. So you can't escape.

TRIXIE. Twenty miles south of 'ere, pal.

NELL. Y'sure? You sure I ain't going there?

HANNAH. You spoke to the man from Sterling, Nell. Mr
    Cholerton. 'E explained 'ow you're workin' wi' them an'
    staying wi' us.

NELL. Making explosives?

ADA. Telephony.

GLADYS. For the Royal Air Force an' the Navy.

JAMES. So long as you toe the line. (*Nods to the vegetables.*) An' pull your weight in the 'ouse.

HANNAH. Father…

JAMES *leaves, followed by* HANNAH. NELL *takes a moment to absorb his words.*

NELL. I'm a servant.

GLADYS. You'll 'elp out but we all do that.

TRIXIE. When we can. We're out at half-five in the morning.

NELL (*nods to the bike*). On that?

ADA. Saves a three-mile walk there an' back.

NELL. But I can't though, I've never…

TRIXIE. Well, maybe dear Ada'll teach ya?

ADA. It's you need teaching.

GLADYS. Lots o'girls cycle round 'ere.

TRIXIE. Got the wages to spend on 'em, see?

GLADYS. An' it wards off diseases: rheumatics, nerves, varicose veins –

NELL. Influenza?

GLADYS. Well, that's a virus but –

TRIXIE. Fresh air an' exercise, that's what you'll find 'ere.

ADA. Country air.

NELL. Country air you can breathe.

ADA. Games an' sports.

NELL. Sports?

GLADYS. Singing an' dancing.

TRIXIE. Making hay while the sun shines!

NELL. I thought it was war work.

GLADYS. It is but…

ADA. Ain't all it is.

NELL. I just wanna – I've come for a better – that's why I'm –
I just want more than I got.

4.

Maya's home. Alone in the house, MAYA *listens to* Grass in the
Clouds, *a football podcast. Its presenters are* IDA SHEPHERD
and SOPHIE JONES.

IDA. Hi, I'm Ida Shepherd.

SOPHIE. I'm Sophie Jones.

IDA. And you're listening to *Grass in the Clouds*, the go-to
podcast for all things women's football.

SOPHIE. In this episode, we're taking a deep-dive into anterior
cruciate ligament injury: what, how and crucially, why it's
reached epidemic levels.

IDA. If you're currently down an' out of the game, you're not
alone.

SOPHIE. Grassroots or Lioness, let's talk ACL.

5.

Sports ground. A Saturday in July. Warm applause as Managing Director GUY BURNEY *takes the podium. He is flanked by Assistant Works Manager* ED CHOLERTON (CHOLLY) *and factory worker* MAUD READER, *in cricket whites.* NELL *is watching with* ADA, GLADYS *and* TRIXIE.

BURNEY. Ladies and gentlemen, supporters and friends. I am delighted to welcome you on this glorious summer afternoon to the ceremonial opening of the Sterling Sports and Social Club Ground.

GLADYS (*to* NELL). Mr Burney. Our Managing Director.

BURNEY. Having established a first-class Athletic Club here on Rainham Road, we were successful in acquiring some five acres of land to be used solely for recreational pursuits. We gratefully acknowledge the generous financial assistance of our board of directors, and the – dare I say – 'sterling' work of our Sports and Social Committee, embodied here in the fine form of our chairman...

GLADYS. Mr Cholerton.

CHOLLY. I'm not sure about the fine form these days, sir.

GLADYS. Assistant Works Manager.

NELL. I know.

BURNEY. Representing our female workforce, I am also delighted to share the podium with sporting stalwart and Becontree Heath girl, Maud Reader.

A wolf-whistle for an embarrassed MAUD.

ADA. Lives at The Merry Fiddler.

NELL. Whass' that?

TRIXIE. A pub. Run by 'er family.

GLADYS. We work together, Machine Room.

BURNEY. Now, there's a feeling in England that capital and labour cannot – some say must not – combine. This is not a view we hold. We stand 'as one' for King and Country, knowing the more determined and united our individual efforts, the sooner the joy-bells of victory will ring!

Applause.

Until that day, we pledge to do all we can to promote your health and happiness in these testing times. Be it field or track, sport not only strengthens our body and mind but our sense of belonging and our will to win!

Applause.

Our two thousand employees unite in the spirit of fair play: courage, justice, wisdom and parity. With this in mind, I invite Miss Reader to share an extract from a letter I received from the Romford Member of Parliament no less, Sir John Bethell.

MAUD (*reads a note*). 'Formerly known as "the gentle sex", the women of Romford, Dagenham and beyond have proved themselves equal not only on the factory floor but the highly competitive field of sport. If our Sterling Ladies make majority use of your marvellous facility, I for one will be cheering them on!'

Applause, slightly muted by MAUD*'s delivery.*

TRIXIE. Lord 'elp us.

GLADYS. Leave 'er.

BURNEY. So, without further ado… On Saturday June 16th in the year of our Lord 1917, I proudly declare the Sterling Sports and Social Club Ground open and free for all time!

BURNEY *snips the ribbon. Applause as the band strikes up a sporting song in celebration. As* BURNEY *shakes hands,* MAUD *sees* GLADYS, ADA *and* TRIXIE *watching her. They commentate on the action as they see it.*

TRIXIE. Go on, gal.

ADA. Get in there.

GLADYS. Now's your chance.

As BURNEY *turns to go*, MAUD *pipes up*.

MAUD. Sir?

TRIXIE. Yes!

MAUD *gestures for them to clear off and turns back to* BURNEY.

MAUD. May I... May I have a word?

6.

MAYA *is listening to* Grass in the Clouds.

SOPHIE. Then for most of us, there's the issue of waiting lists.

IDA. Cos if you're Chloe Kelly – devastating though it is – you're straight into surgery, intensive rehab –

SOPHIE. Twelve months and you're playing again.

IDA. But if you don't have insurance, it's year or more just for the op.

MAYA. Thirteen months.

IDA. What does that do to you, psychologically?

SOPHIE. It's so, so tough. Cos in terms of recovery, surgery's only the start.

7.

Sports ground. Moments later. MAUD *puts her case to*
BURNEY *and* CHOLLY.

MAUD. It began as shop-floor banter, sir. A kick-about in the
yard. The gals were keen to follow it through. All told, we
played three times this year.

BURNEY. 'We' being…

MAUD. Assembly Room verses Machine Room. Twice in March,
once in April. Spirited, hard-fought games. As Mr Cholerton
can attest from the last.

BURNEY. Really?

CHOLLY. I was referee-come-ringmaster, sir.

MAUD. Ringmaster?

CHOLLY. It *was* a bit of a circus, Miss Reader.

MAUD. You calling us clowns, sir?

BURNEY. I'm sure what Mr Cholerton means is… (*Turns.*)
What *do* you mean?

CHOLLY. Organised but highly entertaining chaos.

MAUD. The *Barking Recorder* don't think so.

BURNEY. Oh?

MAUD. 'A rare spectacle', that's what they wrote. 'By the
talented ladies.'

BURNEY. Bravo!

MAUD. The girls 'ave talked about nothing else since. An'
they've asked me to ask you – on their behalf – if we can
form a team?

CHOLLY. A football team.

MAUD. Sterling Ladies.

BURNEY. To play Sterling Men? (*To* CHOLLY.) Well, I'm sure
that could be arranged.

CHOLLY. It's not quite a level playing field, sir.

BURNEY. The chaps can turn out in fancy dress. Play with their hands tied.

CHOLLY. I'll get on to it.

BURNEY. Good man!

Exit BURNEY. MAUD *raises her game.*

MAUD. Mr Cholerton? With respect, that ain't what we want.

CHOLLY. What, a handicap?

MAUD. Marconi and Hoffmann's 'ave ladies' teams. They met each other in June. Drew a crowd of two thousand, raised twenty pounds on the gate for the Red Cross Hospital.

CHOLLY. Twenty?

MAUD. Brocks Laundry, they call 'em the Romford Girls. Played Hoffmann's an' beat 'em three–two. There's rumours Vickers are fielding a side from Crayford an' Dartford combined.

CHOLLY. Combined? That's some firepower.

MAUD. The girls believe we can punch above. If Marconi raised twenty pounds, we'll double it. Treble it.

CHOLLY. What makes you so confident, Miss Reader?

MAUD. We all played as kids on Nanny Goat Common. We're doing men's work on men's hours. Not for men's wages, of course but –

CHOLLY. That's not for today.

MAUD. We're 'equal not only on the factory floor but the field of sport'. An actual MP says that, so…

CHOLLY. I'll put it to the committee.

MAUD. Would you train us?

CHOLLY. If the committee agree, yes, we'd find you –

MAUD. Won't *you* train us, sir?

Beat.

CHOLLY. Why would I?

MAUD. You refereed.

CHOLLY. I was roped in, yes.

MAUD. You know the game. You played in goal for Romford Town.

CHOLLY. Way back.

MAUD. With Ernest Fairman. His sister Gladys says you were good.

CHOLLY. Well, that's very nice of her but –

MAUD. Will yer? Please?

8.

MAYA *is listening to* Grass in the Clouds.

SOPHIE. What do I take from all this? That making a conscious decision to be optimistic is one of the biggest steps forward.

IDA. And to see the likes of Chloe Kelly – who's been to hell and back mentally – recovered and playing again.

SOPHIE. Scoring the winner at the Euros.

IDA. Shows there's light at the end of the tunnel.

SOPHIE. Absolutely. However dark it gets, there is hope.

9.

Sports ground. Later that day. Tied together at the ankle,
ADA *and* TRIXIE *practise for a three-legged race. Moving in an*
opposing circle, NELL *trains for an egg-and-spoon race.*
ADA *and* TRIXIE *sing 'When Tommy Comes Marching Home'*
to keep them in rhythm. As they sing, GLADYS *directs the traffic.*

GLADYS. Tied foot forward!

ADA *and* TRIXIE.
    The girls were crying their eyes out
    When the Tommys went off to war
    But the girls will all be smiling
    When they see 'em come back once more –

GLADYS. Left, Nell! To the left!

    NELL *swerves around* ADA *and* TRIXIE, *still singing.*

    Tied foot forward – in balance, in rhythm, that's it! Keep it up!

ADA *and* TRIXIE.
    You'll see the ladies Maud and Lou
    With the boys in khaki blue
    But they'll never be short of a fag or two
    When Tommy comes marching –

NELL. Oi!

    As NELL *comes around,* TRIXIE *and* ADA *swerve and*
    stumble.

ADA. Watch it!

NELL. You watch it!

GLADYS. Keep going, keep –

TRIXIE. Aw!

    TRIXIE *and* ADA *take a tumble.*

GLADYS. Useless!

ADA. Do you wanna try it?

GLADYS. I'm saving meself for the wheelbarrow race.

TRIXIE. Remind us why? Remind us please why we'd ever agree to this?

ADA. Nell.

GLADYS. Don't say it like that.

ADA. Cos Ma ordered us to bring 'er down.

TRIXIE. For silly kids' games?

GLADYS. For exercise. She's got a weak chest.

NELL *circles past, her eyes fixed on the egg.*

NELL. Shift!

ADA. Weak? She's as tough as old boots.

TRIXIE. Smells like 'em, an' all.

GLADYS. Oi! It's a bit o' fun an' it gets 'er involved.

ADA. It *was* fun. Every day till she turned up.

GLADYS. She's shy, that's all. But we 'ave a little chinwag in bed.

ADA. 'Bout what?

GLADYS. Ma and Pa, how they met.

ADA. You've told 'er?

GLADYS. Why not? Ain't a secret.

TRIXIE. He's married, widowed an' left with a little 'un. Takes on your ma as 'ousekeeper-nursemaid but soon enough –

ADA. Tell the 'ole world, why don't ya?

TRIXIE. I'm family, aren't I?!

ADA. Not quite.

TRIXIE (*sings*).
  When Ernest comes marching home again
  Hoorah, hurrah –

ADA. Father thinks you've forgotten 'im.

TRIXIE. Beg your pardon?

MAUD *appears, carrying a football.*

MAUD. Well, it's all kickin' off.

NELL *comes around again. Stops to listen.* TRIXIE *and* ADA *rally.*

GLADYS. Burney said yes?

MAUD. 'E did.

GLADYS. Yes!

MAUD. To fancy-dress football.

NELL. Football?

MAUD. An' Cholerton don't wanna train us.

TRIXIE. Why not?

MAUD. Too busy.

GLADYS. Busy? He's a bachelor.

MAUD. At work, so 'e says.

TRIXIE. Aren't we all?

MAUD. Says anyway it ain't up to 'im, it's for the committee to –

ADA. When do they next meet?

MAUD. October.

TRIXIE. That's three months.

GLADYS. An' if they say no?

MAUD. He's kiboshed it for us all.

Beat.

TRIXIE. Typical, ain't it? He'll 'ave a laugh an' a joke on the shop-floor but –

ADA. End of the day, 'e's management.

MAUD. I tried to say that's what we need. A manager, like the men's team. Who knows the game, who –

NELL. Never said nothin' to me.

GLADYS. Cholerton?

ADA. Why would 'e?

NELL. 'E took us on, didn't 'e? Asked what me interests… if 'e'd a'said football…

GLADYS. You played?

TRIXIE. Where?

NELL. On cobblestones, horseshit and piss.

ADA. Know what? I've 'ad enough o'your mouth?

TRIXIE. Ada –

NELL. An' I've 'ad enough o'your face.

ADA. 'Ave yer? 'Ave yer!

　　ADA *squares up to* NELL. *As she does,* CHOLLY *crosses.*

NELL. Yep!

　　NELL *breaks her egg on* ADA*'s forehead.*

ADA. Ow –

NELL. Next time it's your 'ead –

GLADYS. She asked for that –

CHOLLY. What's this –

ADA. She's a lunatic, that's what!

CHOLLY. Enough!

　　CHOLLY *puts himself between* NELL *and* ADA.

NELL. She started it.

TRIXIE (*to* ADA). Come 'ere! Now!

　　TRIXIE *takes* ADA *away to clean her up.* CHOLLY *turns to* NELL.

CHOLLY. Miss Marchant.

NELL. She 'ad it comin' an' what's going on?

CHOLLY. I beg your pardon?

NELL. Wi' you? Why won't you let gals play?

All eyes are now on CHOLLY *and* NELL. *He glances at* MAUD. *Turns to* NELL.

CHOLLY. Young lady: when the Labour Exchange referred you to us, you said to me – and I quote – you 'had nothing and nowhere to go'.

NELL. Don't send us back.

CHOLLY. You'd scraped a living from lace work, cleaning, matchbox-making.

NELL. In filthy factories for tuppence a week.

CHOLLY. At Sterling, you earn rather more than tuppence. You lodge with a fine local family. But if you persist in that kind of behaviour, you'll lose your place here and there. Which nobody wants, do they?

NELL. She does. (*Points to* ADA.) That one.

CHOLLY. To whom you owe an apology.

CHOLLY *holds firm until* NELL *begrudgingly answers.*

NELL. Sorry.

GLADYS. Don't rise to it, Ada.

TRIXIE. Don't egg 'er on.

ADA *catches the twinkle in* TRIXIE's *eye.* MAUD *is watching a surly* NELL.

CHOLLY. You're competing today, Miss Marchant?

NELL. Egg-and-spoon race.

CHOLLY. Good.

NELL. They think it's all I can do.

CHOLLY. Games and sports are a healthy way to divert our anger – channel our energies – turn a dark feeling to light.

NELL. Like football.

TRIXIE (*aside*). Aye-aye.

CHOLLY. Football, yes. When we've found the right chap to –

NELL. They want you.

MAUD (*aside*). You tell 'im.

ADA. We wanna play properly, sir. That's all.

TRIXIE. We wanna play well.

GLADYS. An' if we can't play now, we're thinking, well… when?

CHOLLY. Now's the time, yes, I see that, Miss Fairman. (*Beat*.) But I'm sorry, I'm not the man.

   NELL *grabs a football*.

NELL. West Ham United, y'know 'em?

CHOLLY. Of course.

NELL. The Boleyn Ground, Upton Park? S'were I was born and me brother, he knew how to nip in wi'out being seen. So we did.

GLADYS. You've a brother?

NELL. Saw Syd Puddefoot score five, we did. FA Cup.

CHOLLY. You were there?

NELL. Danny Shea, before 'e went to –

CHOLLY. Blackburn Rovers. For two thousand pounds.

GLADYS. Where is he now?

NELL. Shea? At war, I suppose.

GLADYS. Your brother?

NELL. Dead an' gone. (*Takes a moment*.) Till I've a ball at me feet.

NELL *dribbles into the space, flips the ball in the air and starts kick-ups with one foot.*

Her skills are ragged but her balance and concentration are sharp as a tack.

CHOLLY. Both feet?

NELL *shifts to kicking with alternative feet but doesn't get as far.*

Tap it up, that's all. Don't swing just…

NELL (*flips the ball onto her knees*). One-two-one-two-one-two –

CHOLLY. Arms out for balance …

NELL *falters after a few bounces.*

Again.

NELL. Your turn.

NELL *throws the ball to* CHOLLY. GLADYS, ADA *and* TRIXIE *watch him. He evades their eyes.*

CHOLLY. October 1912. Cup game wi' Catford, quarter-final. Goal-mouth scramble, I dive in, their thug of a striker stamps on my hand with his studs. Shatters my thumb and two fingers, they don't mend right…

NELL. That why you ain't in France?

CHOLLY. When you can't fire a mortar, pull a trigger, lift a stretcher…

NELL. You can still kick a ball.

CHOLLY. How? (*Beat.*) When the team, the boys – brothers, husbands, sweethearts – are out there an' I'm…

GLADYS. S'alright, sir…

NELL. But we're not the boys.

GLADYS. Nell –

NELL. Mister? We're the gals.

10.

Maya's home. Friday July 28th. Mid-morning. Airpods in,
MAYA *is intensely focused on her phone. As she watches*
England vs Denmark, SAMMY *comes in. Watches* MAYA *for*
a moment or two.

COMMENTARY (*voice-over*). Captain Millie Bright steps up
for Leah Williamson. Bronze. Nice play move Russo to get
there. Walsh. James. That's Lauren James – OH!!

  MAYA *registers the beauty, thrill and significance of the*
  goal.

SAMMY. Three weeks today, gal.

COMMENTARY (*voice-over*). It all comes together for
England!

SAMMY. It's coming.

COMMENTARY (*voice-over*). Lauren James!

SAMMY. The first day of the rest of your life.

COMMENTARY (*voice-over*). Magnificent!

SAMMY. Maya!

MAYA. What?

  MAYA *takes her airpods out.*

SAMMY. You live on that phone.

MAYA. You can talk.

SAMMY. I'd like to. I'd love to talk if you weren't wherever
you are.

MAYA. I'm 'ere. 108 Park Lane, Hornchurch.

SAMMY. From whence I'm trying to work.

MAYA. Whence?

SAMMY. We got the instruction – three doors down – in case
you're wondering?

MAYA. No.

SAMMY. Goes on Rightmove tomorrow. If they get the asking price, I might be next.

MAYA. What d'you mean?

SAMMY. Well, as I was saying, three weeks today, you'll have your results. An' then…?

MAYA. I'll have my results.

SAMMY. Empty nest? I might downsize. Garden flat, 'undred-K in the bank.

MAYA. Hang on, I've not got a place.

SAMMY. Clearing, Maya? If your grades are higher than predicted –

MAYA. I'm 'aving a gap year.

SAMMY. Don't mean we can't do some research into courses. Make a list, put them in priority order.

MAYA. Now?

SAMMY. Fail to prepare, prepare to fail.

MAYA. I'm not a failure!

Beat.

SAMMY. I know that. You've worked so hard this year: on your schoolwork, your self-esteem.

MAYA. An' that's why I want a year out. To…

SAMMY. Do what, exactly? You got ideas? You know how you'll pay for a gap year?

MAYA. Me trust fund.

SAMMY. Funny.

MAYA. I'll work. I'll look for a job.

SAMMY. You said that in June.

MAYA. I'll keep looking.

SAMMY. Or try volunteering, perhaps?

MAYA. For the UCAS form?

SAMMY. For a sense of fulfilment.

MAYA. I am fulfilled.

SAMMY. Watching England–Denmark on your iPhone?

Beat.

MAYA. I was checking the score.

SAMMY. Score's right, you're sneaking round like you're on drugs.

MAYA. That's it, do what you always do, make it a Massive Thing.

SAMMY. Why can't you tell me? Why can't you say when it's causing you such –

MAYA. Cos it causes you more!

SAMMY. Know what upsets me? To see you still thinking if you ain't the one per cent you're… When y'can do anything y'put your mind to, Maya. You can be whatever you wanna be, right?

MAYA. Thing is, though, you can't.

SAMMY. 'There is nothing either good or bad but thinking makes it so.' Who said that?

MAYA. Sarina Wiegman.

SAMMY. Hamlet.

MAYA. A made-up person.

SAMMY. A Danish person.

MAYA. Who never played academy football. Who was never released.

SAMMY. You were injured. You weren't given time to recover, you're still recovering an' once you 'ave –

MAYA. Don't matter. Door's closed. It's over an' done with.

SAMMY. You reckon? There's all kinds of courses: sports science, coaching, administration, journalism –

MAYA. It's over.

SAMMY. What's the score? England, they winning?

MAYA. One–nil. Lauren James, five minutes in.

SAMMY. Let's watch.

MAYA. You're working.

SAMMY. From 'ome. Got me phone. Big screen, let's watch it together.

SAMMY *flicks the TV on.* MAYA *reluctantly moves back into the room.*

COMMENTARY (*voice-over*). Did someone call her Reece's sister?

SAMMY. One–nil, still.

COMMENTARY (*voice-over*). Nope, he's Lauren's brother.

MAYA. Too right.

SAMMY *and* MAYA *watch together.*

COMMENTARY (*voice-over*). England take possession. Keira Walsh. James. Russo. Bronze. Lovely run by Lucy Bronze…

SAMMY. Game plan's working?

MAYA. That's Sarina. She knows how to change an' adapt; shuffle the pack, stay unpredictable.

COMMENTARY (*voice-over*). James tries to reach Kelly but they're cut out by Denmark.

MAYA. 'Old up?

SAMMY. What?

MAYA. She's down.

COMMENTARY (*voice-over*). What's happened here?

SAMMY. Who?

MAYA. She's off the ball and...

COMMENTARY (*voice-over*). Oh, I don't like the look of it one little bit.

SAMMY. Keira Walsh?

COMMENTARY (*voice-over*). Oh dear.

MAYA. She was running an' then...

COMMENTARY (*voice-over*). We see now, her studs, they're caught in the ground...

SAMMY. ACL?

COMMENTARY (*voice-over*). They turn one way, she goes the other...

MAYA. No.

COMMENTARY (*voice-over*). She's over...

SAMMY. ACL.

MAYA. We don't know that.

SAMMY. I think we do.

COMMENTARY (*voice-over*). This, of course, is a live conversation in women's football.

MAYA. No...

COMMENTARY (*voice-over*). But whatever it is, Keira Walsh can't go on.

MAYA *lets out a cry of anguish.* SAMMY *switches the match off.*

SAMMY. That's enough of that.

MAYA. What?!

SAMMY. See why I don't want you watching?

MAYA. See why I don't want *you* to?

SAMMY. Right – okay – we need to discuss this. We need to talk about the injury, the academy –

MAYA. We 'ave. Back then, me an' them. Took 'em five minutes to say: 'Oh, thanks for the last six years but we'll help you adjust, we'll support you in finding a pathway.'

SAMMY. Let's get this straight. You were released not rejected.

MAYA. What's the difference?

SAMMY. Rejected: thrown out. Released? Set free.

MAYA. Free of what?

SAMMY. All this 'follow your dream' stuff for starters.

MAYA. It actually wasn't a dream. It was real-life training, studying, working –

SAMMY. At the expense of your schoolwork.

MAYA. Oh, here we go.

SAMMY. It was a great achievement, Maya. To get selected –

MAYA. A career.

SAMMY. For heaven's sake, you were nine when you signed.

MAYA. An' I knew what I wanted.

MAYA *puts the TV on.*

I knew.

COMMENTARY (*voice-over*). This could be a catastrophic turn of events, for Keira Walsh and for England. Let's not speculate too much but it's troubling… very troubling indeed.

11.

Sports ground. A week or so later. CHOLLY *leads* ADA, GLADYS, TRIXIE *and* NELL *in a militaristic Swedish Drill.*

CHOLLY. Hips – firm. Attention!

The women adopt standing position: feet outwards, arms straight. Their movements will follow his commands. As the routine unfolds, it speeds up.

Head to left turn –
Head forward –
Head to right turn –
Head forward –

It's a familiar routine to all but NELL.

Head erect – eyes front – arms straight – heels together.
Wing-standing!

Hands on hips and feet together.

Arms across – bend!

Arms raise and fingers touch across the chest.

One-two-one-two-one-two-one-two-one-two-one-two-one-two-one-two-one-two-one-two-one-two.

Arms pump up and down across the chest.

Attention!

Return to standing position.

Neck-rest.

(*To* NELL.) Hands behind head, fingers interlock…

Head straight and elbows back.

NELL *takes her orders. The routine goes into fifth gear.*

Left hand neck-rest; right hand, hips – firm!
Arms-change!
And change! And change!
And change! And change!

ALL. Change! Change! Change! Change!

CHOLLY. Fly!

The women flap their arms as if they're about to take off.

Fly!

ALL. Change! Change! Change –

CHOLLY. Attention!

Somewhat breathless, the women stand to attention.

Stand easy.

The women deflate as they catch their breath.

ADA. Easy?

NELL (*gasping*). 'Tis.

TRIXIE. At six at night off a twelve-hour shift?

GLADYS. An' I've still got to cycle home. (*To* NELL.) Y'alright?

NELL. Course.

CHOLLY (*briskly*). Swedish Drill. A therapeutic system of gymnastics first learned in school.

TRIXIE. Reform School.

CHOLLY. Enlivens, invigorates, lifts the spirits. Instils self-discipline, body and mind –

ADA. Ain't it football we're here for?

TRIXIE. Ball-kick-net?

GLADYS. Proper football.

ADA. Well, some of us are, where's the Merry Fiddler?

GLADYS. Eleven-a-side.

CHOLLY. Doesn't matter, we –

ADA. Even though only us four.

NELL. Can y'shut your traps an' let Cholly talk!

ADA. Cholly?

TRIXIE (*laughs*). Who's Cholly?

NELL. Our manager.

CHOLLY. I'm not. I'm gettin' you goin', that's all.

TRIXIE. Aye-aye?!

CHOLLY. An' four's fine for now. Four's a foundation.

NELL. Ain't a team though, Cholly.

GLADYS. Mr Cholerton.

NELL. At work. (*To* CHOLLY.) But we're not now, are we?

> CHOLLY *keeps a straight face but there's a smile in his eyes.*

CHOLLY. What you say out of earshot is of no concern but until we can dupe someone else into doing it, you may address me as Gaffer.

NELL. Gaffer.

> TRIXIE *and* ADA *are starting to laugh.*

CHOLLY. You'll be glad to know the Sports and Social Committee are contacting works' teams in the locality to secure games for the newly formed Sterling Ladies.

TRIXIE (*to* ADA). Five-a-side?

CHOLLY. There's twelve hundred women work here. When word gets around, you'll have to fight for your place in a season which so far has ties with Brocks Laundry, Burton Vowles Shirtmakers and Sopwith.

ADA. What about Vickers?

GLADYS. Marconi.

CHOLLY. Let's not bite off more than we can chew, ladies.

TRIXIE. Or pass a ball straight, Ada Fairman.

ADA. Excuse me, I scored twice in three games.

NELL. Matches.

GLADYS. Only cos I let yer.

ADA. Why would yer?

GLADYS. Pity.

CHOLLY. Anyway!

    MAUD *runs to join them.*

MAUD. S'alright, I'm 'ere now.

TRIXIE. Too late.

ADA. You've lost your place to a passin' duck.

MAUD. I were stopped in the yard by Mr Burney.

CHOLLY. Really?

MAUD. Or 'is car, should I say?

TRIXIE. 'E ran you down?

CHOLLY. Quiet!

MAUD. Chauffeur stopped an' 'e's sat in the back. Says: 'Now then, Miss Reader? I've news on the football front.'

TRIXIE. We're playing at West Ham?

ADA. Dream on.

NELL. Shut up.

MAUD. 'My wife has shown rather an interest.'

GLADYS. She don't wanna play?

NELL. She's ancient!

ADA. She's forty, tops.

NELL. Ancient.

MAUD. 'She has a connection at Harrods of Knightsbridge. She spoke of our Sterling Ladies and you'll never guess? They're keen to secure a game.'

TRIXIE. With us?

GLADYS. Never!

ADA. What are we gonna wear?

CHOLLY. Sterling Men's away kit. Blue-and-white-quartered shirts. De rigueur, so I'm told. It's sorted.

ADA. Can we make alterations? Take 'em in? They'll be more like a dress if we don't.

NELL. Who cares 'ow it looks? Y'get into position an' play.

NELL *picks up a football.*

ADA. Just like that?

NELL. Like this. Keeper, two halfbacks, one fullback. Rest are forwards cos that's what you do. Go forward. Boot the ball upfield an' follow the gal what gets it. Stick yer Swedish Drill up yer arse. Shoot. Score.

NELL *silences the field.*

CHOLLY. What's that in your hand, Miss Marchant?

NELL. Nell.

CHOLLY. Try again?

NELL. A football. If you don't know by now.

CHOLLY. Once more.

NELL. A pig's fat bladder in leather, you tell us.

NELL *throws the ball to* CHOLLY. *He places it in the palm of his hands.*

CHOLLY. This, girls, is your pride and joy. The greatest prize you have; the most precious thing you own. Cos that's what you do out there. All of you. Own the ball. Take possession – share possession – keep possession. Care for it, protect it, love it. That's it, that's all. That's football.

TRIXIE. How?

CHOLLY. Football's a game of invasion: defence and attack. An' in my view, it's fought best with teamwork and discipline *on the ground*. Not by one girl running with ten behind her, Nell. By the full eleven, holding formation and passing the ball. By the clean, attractive, possession-based, counter-attacking style that Sterling Men an' their ilk can't… See, they play what's called the Pyramid System.

NELL. Five at the back.

CHOLLY. The long ball. Hoofing it up over everyone's heads and a free-for-all when it falls. Defensive, aggressive play; two-footed tackles with studs-up. That's not what you do. Cos if God meant you to play in the sky, girls, he'd'a put grass on the clouds.

NELL. Good one.

CHOLLY. No. There's another way to do this; a better way.

NELL. What?

CHOLLY. An eleven-strong team. Side by side. Keeper, fullbacks, wingers, sweeper, striker. Playing together, tight as a drum. Dribbling, passing, and finding the space. Stay wide and move forward. Look forward. Soaking up the pressure, a lightning-quick break and… (*As if seeing a vision.*)

NELL. Goal.

CHOLLY. Fluid, creative, expressive. That's us.

   CHOLLY *feels the weight of the 'us'. Will he continue?*

Cos we play for the love of the game, girls. We play for the love of the game.

12.

CHOLLY *paces the touchline and* MAYA *watches television. Our focus moves between them as Sterling Ladies vs Burton Vowles plays out to the England vs China commentary. As* MAYA *lives the game, so does* CHOLLY. *The England goals and incidents become Sterling's story.* MAYA *shouts at the TV,* CHOLLY *to the players.*

CHOLLY. Here we go, girls.

COMMENTARY (*voice-over*). Here we go!

CHOLLY. Sterling Ladies v Burton Vowles.

MAYA. England v China.

COMMENTARY (*voice-over*). England take on China. All they need is a draw and they're through to the Group Stage.

CHOLLY. First game. We've everything to play for and nothing to lose.

MAYA. Three-four-one-two.

CHOLLY. Teamwork: that's how it starts and ends, right? Go out there and play for each other. Nicely done, Peters!

COMMENTARY (*voice-over*). Welcome back to Lauren Hemp.

MAYA. Three-four-one-two formation, how's that gonna work?

CHOLLY. Good.

COMMENTARY (*voice-over*). Oh, Stanway's lost possession.

CHOLLY. Never mind, Reader. Up you get, up you get!

COMMENTARY (*voice-over*). Both on yellow cards of course – Hemp and Stanway – one more, they're suspended.

MAYA. Back three high and wide…

COMMENTARY (*voice-over*). England…

MAYA. Can join the attack…

CHOLLY. Fairman's in space, she's in plenty of space… yes!

COMMENTARY (*voice-over*). Daly.

MAYA. Yeh, it's looking…

CHOLLY. Keep possession.

COMMENTARY (*voice-over*). Keeping possession.

CHOLLY. Lovely work, Peters.

COMMENTARY (*voice-over*). Russo.

MAYA. It's giving her the freedom she wants.

CHOLLY. Keep the tempo, that's it.

COMMENTARY (*voice-over*). Hemp makes her presence felt, now Bronze.

MAYA. Looking good.

CHOLLY. Hold your shape, girls.

MAYA. Hold the shape.

COMMENTARY (*voice-over*). James.

MAYA. James!

CHOLLY. Marchant.

COMMENTARY (*voice-over*). A Russo shot!

CHOLLY. Peters!

MAYA. An' there it is!

COMMENTARY (*voice-over*). Goal!

CHOLLY. Goal!

COMMENTARY (*voice-over*). What more do you need at this stage in the game?

CHOLLY. Three minutes an' counting, Trixie Peters!

COMMENTARY (*voice-over*). Straight ahead for the final sixteen!

MAYA. Ruuuuusssssssoooo!

Sense of the matches existing in a magical and timeless bubble.

COMMENTARY (*voice-over*). Oops, Stanway didn't see that pass coming.

CHOLLY. Well recovered, take your time.

COMMENTARY (*voice-over*). Millie Bright, commanding. James in her sights.

MAYA. Number ten.

COMMENTARY (*voice-over*). Can she make the pass?

MAYA. Yes?

CHOLLY. Yes!

COMMENTARY (*voice-over*). Yes, indeed! Lauren Hemp for England, it's a brilliant finish as well!

MAYA *and* CHOLLY. Two!

COMMENTARY (*voice-over*). Lauren Hemp –

CHOLLY. Ada Fairman!

COMMENTARY (*voice-over*). Firing on all cylinders, England.

CHOLLY. Play up, the Sterling!

COMMENTARY (*voice-over*). A change in shape; it's a work of art!

MAYA. Ain't it?!

COMMENTARY (*voice-over*). And still, they press forward.

CHOLLY. Organise, girls.

COMMENTARY (*voice-over*). Greenwood and Zelem… Lauren James in plenty of space…

MAYA. To James –

CHOLLY. To Marchant –

COMMENTARY (*voice-over*). TO JAMES!!

CHOLLY. MARCHANT!

COMMENTARY (*voice-over*). And there she goes!

MAYA. Job done, we're through.

COMMENTARY (*voice-over*). It's an open road to the knockouts for England.

MAYA. Handball?

CHOLLY. Penalty?

MAYA. Never?

CHOLLY. Focus, girls.

MAYA. Well, for what it's worth.

COMMENTARY (*voice-over*). Penalty for China! Shuang Wang. Scores!

CHOLLY. On your feet, goalie. Chin up.

MAYA. You'll not trouble Earps again.

COMMENTARY (*voice-over*). Coombs. Carter. Bronze. Carter.

CHOLLY. Saggers – Foster – Hale.

COMMENTARY (*voice-over*). James is available.

CHOLLY. Marchant.

COMMENTARY (*voice-over*). Oh, my!! You can't better that.

CHOLLY. Yeeeeessss!

COMMENTARY (*voice-over*). Pure Jamesian magic!

MAYA. Phenomenal.

COMMENTARY (*voice-over*). Kelly steams in…!

MAYA. Boom!!

COMMENTARY (*voice-over*). Five–one England.

CHOLLY. Five… five!

COMMENTARY (*voice-over*). Chloe Kelly on the scoresheet, England's confidence rising.

CHOLLY. Heads high, girls! Heads high!

COMMENTARY (*voice-over*). And so it should. Step forward the group winners!

MAYA (*feels it deeply*). Wow.

CHOLLY. Cool heads now.

COMMENTARY (*voice-over*). Toone.

CHOLLY. Hale.

COMMENTARY (*voice-over*). Charles.

CHOLLY. Billet.

COMMENTARY (*voice-over*). Neat ball from Kelly.

CHOLLY. Mullet.

COMMENTARY (*voice-over*). Tricky from Toone. Kelly!

CHOLLY. Reader!

MAYA. Daly!

COMMENTARY (*voice-over*). Rachel Daly, you can't keep her down.

MAYA. Perfection.

COMMENTARY (*voice-over*). Six goals on the scoresheet as England dominate!

MAYA (*raises a fist*). Six–one, yes.

COMMENTARY (*voice-over*). Topping the group. Brisbane-bound.

MAYA (*fist to heart*). Yes.

CHOLLY. Magnificent, girls. Just…

COMMENTARY (*voice-over*). A quarter-final clash with Nigeria next but the final score here –

CHOLLY. Sterling six – Burton Vowles one.

13.

Fairman home. A Saturday in September. Still in their kit, ADA, GLADYS *and* NELL *tumble in after their victory over Burton Vowles.* NELL *is limping. They sing the score to the tune of 'Amazing Grace' as* HANNAH *comes in to meet them.*

ADA, GLADYS *and* NELL. Six–one, six–one, six–one, six–one, six–one, six–one, six–one!

HANNAH. Six to who?

ADA, GLADYS *and* NELL. Six–one, six–one, six–one, six–one, six–one, six–one, six–one!

HANNAH. You?

GLADYS. Oh, Ma…

ADA. It was… I ain't got the words.

GLADYS. Y'don't need 'em. Score speaks for itself.

NELL. We stuffed 'em.

HANNAH. I 'ope not.

ADA. Burton Vowles – the Shirtmakers – We ripped 'em apart!

GLADYS. Ran 'em ragged!

HANNAH. But it's not how you win, girls. It's how you play the game.

NELL. Four-four-two.

HANNAH. Four-four…?

NELL. That's how we play. Like Cholly says, y'build from the back.

HANNAH. Cholly?

ADA. Mr Cholerton.

HANNAH. Y'don't call him that to his face?

ADA. He likes it. Makes out he don't but he does.

NELL. See, it starts with yer keeper.

GLADYS. Safe pair of hands.

ADA. Last line of defence.

GLADYS. She soaks up the pressure, reads the game an' launches attacks with a kick an' a throw.

HANNAH. Nell –

NELL. Yer fullbacks sit deep and play forward. Big gals who can tackle, mark, 'ead.

HANNAH. You limping?

ADA. Our wing-backs –

GLADYS. Workhorses. Stamina, pace, acceleration. Young legs who are fast but don't wanna dribble.

HANNAH. You've not 'urt yourself, 'ave yer?

ADA. Centre-midfield, that's me. Defence and attack. Intercept, win the ball; mark, tackle, poach, pass. Sit deep with the back four, then spring.

NELL. Centre-forward.

ADA. Trixie Peters.

GLADYS. Cool and composed. Great dribbler, good legs, knows how to put the ball in the net.

NELL. An' all of us in it together. Attackers, defend. Defenders, attack.

GLADYS. Stay wide. Keep possession.

ADA *and* GLADYS. Pass, pass, pass!

NELL. Score!

HANNAH. Nell, what's up wi' your foot?

ADA. Six, Ma! Six!

NELL. It's sore, thass' all.

ADA. An' who d'you think scored twice?

HANNAH. Take your boot off, let's 'ave a look.

ADA. First from a corner, second a thirty-yard strike.

GLADYS. Ten-yard.

HANNAH. Nell?

ADA. At least it didn't go through the keeper's legs.

GLADYS. I gave 'em that one to soften the blow.

 NELL *does as she's told.*

HANNAH. What on earth?

 NELL *has rolled her socks off and is now starting to pull off a makeshift bandage.*

NELL. I'm a winger, see? Down the touchline. I stays wide an' runs at 'em as fast as I can but me boots…

HANNAH. Your work boots.

NELL. 'Alf-cripple us.

HANNAH. Let's see.

 HANNAH *unravels the bandage from* NELL*'s foot.*

ADA. We told her, Ma. I said to her: 'Go get a pair.'

NELL. Can't afford 'em.

ADA. You're working.

NELL. I gotta save – aw!

HANNAH. S'alright.

GLADYS. S'alright training but a full match –

ADA. No studs, you'll be slippin' an' sliding –

NELL. An' losing me place in the – ah!! (*As* HANNAH *touches the wound.*)

HANNAH. How long 'ave you 'ad this? How long?

NELL. It's only a blister.

ADA. I told 'er.

HANNAH (*to* NELL). An' you shoulda told me.

NELL. I wanted to play.

HANNAH. It's infected.

NELL. I had to play.

HANNAH. You felt feverish?

NELL. No?

HANNAH. Cold, chills? Is your breathin'…

NELL. Normal.

    HANNAH *puts her hands under* NELL*'s chin.*

HANNAH. Your glands…

NELL. What y'doing?

HANNAH. If it goes to your blood.

NELL. It won't.

HANNAH. If we catch it in time.

GLADYS. Salt water?

ADA. A warm, wet cloth.

HANNAH. An' a blanket. Quick as you can.

    GLADYS *and* ADA *spring into action.*

NELL. I had to play.

HANNAH. In work boots?

NELL. I had to.

HANNAH. You tell us, d'you hear? When something like this
    ever happens again, gal…

NELL. It won't.

HANNAH. Tell us.

HANNAH heads into the house. Alone, NELL can't suppress the joy and pain she feels. For a few moments, it is overwhelming.

Through the house comes MAYA. She inhabits her own time and space. She finds a shoebox she's hidden away. Holds it. Dares to open it.

14.

Fairman home. Minutes later. ADA and GLADYS attend to NELL's wounded foot.

GLADYS. Bathe it three times a day, d'you hear? Clean dressings every time.

ADA. An' if you've the merest 'int of a temperature –

NELL. I'll say.

ADA. She don't wanna wake up to you dead in 'er bed.

GLADYS. We want you back to play Brocks.

NELL. Brocks?

GLADYS. Romford Laundry. Munitionettes, most of 'em.

ADA. Rough as.

GLADYS. Now now!

ADA. Loose, Nell. Loose.

GLADYS. Loose tongue.

ADA. Buzzin' like flies round the military base, if y'know what I mean?

GLADYS. They've a Women's Patrol up there keepin' an' eye.

ADA. Sleepy Romford? It's Sodom an' Gomorrah now, pal.

GLADYS (*finishing the job*). There you go.

NELL. Pal?

ADA. Aren't yer?

GLADYS. Patched up an' ready to roll.

NELL. But what am I gonna do sat on me arse?

GLADYS. Backside.

ADA. Derrière.

GLADYS. Practise your reading an' writing.

NELL. On me own?

ADA. Alright, I'll 'elp! We'll start wi' a letter from Ernest.

NELL. Why would I wanna read that? Private, ain't it? Personal.

HANNAH *comes in with a brown paper bag. The sisters know at once what's inside it. She hands it to* NELL.

HANNAH. 'Ere.

NELL. What's this?

HANNAH. Till you've got your own.

GLADYS. Ma…

HANNAH. Open it.

NELL *opens the bag and takes out a pair of pristine leather football boots.*

A couple of sizes too big but needs must…

NELL. Boots?

HANNAH. What d'you think? (*Beat.*) Girls?

GLADYS. With a thick pair of socks…

ADA. Stuff the toes with newspaper.

HANNAH. It's keeping 'em supple an' soft, ey? For when he comes home.

NELL. Ernest?

HANNAH. Go on, Cinderella.

> NELL *knows the significance of the moment. She slips the boots on.* GLADYS *and* ADA *lace them up. In 2023,* MAYA *takes out her treasured boots.* NELL *stands in the studded boots, feeling her way into it.* MAYA *holds them but can't bring herself to put them on.*

GLADYS. Well?

NELL. I've never… Studs, I've not never felt how they…

ADA. Have a walk.

> *As* NELL *walks tentatively across the floor, the studs tap out a rhythm.*

HANNAH. We'll 'ear you coming, that's for sure.

> NELL *looks up.*

NELL. Studs. Boots. Real boots.

> HANNAH *starts to sing 'The Hobnailed Boots That Father Wore', a song they all know from the music halls.*

HANNAH.
Poor Farver's feet took up half the street
So his boots were in proportion
And the kids he'd squash in a day, by gosh
It really was a caution.

> GLADYS *and* ADA *join in.*

GLADYS *and* ADA.
Now me and me brother from the age of four
Up to eleven used to sleep and snore
Nice and cosy in a box of straw –

> NELL *joins in.*

GLADYS, ADA *and* NELL.
In the hobnailed boots that my farver wore.

> NELL *does an impromptu clog dance as she sings. As she does,* JAMES *returns home. For a few seconds, he feels like an intruder.*

NELL.
> In the hobnailed boots that my farver wore
> In the hobnailed boots that my farver –

JAMES. What's this?

The singing stops abruptly.

What y'doing?

JAMES *looks at* NELL*'s feet.*

What's she doin' in them?

JAMES *looks to* HANNAH. ADA, GLADYS *and* NELL
fall silent.

HANNAH. It's Nell. Her name is Nell.

JAMES. That's not what I asked yer.

HANNAH. Girls, would you leave us –

JAMES. Stay where you are.

HANNAH. Father, why don't you and I –

JAMES. What the 'ell is she doin'?

Beat.

HANNAH. I told ya. They've started a team up at work, a girls'
football –

JAMES. Boys play football not girls.

HANNAH. It seems they do now cos they've all been picked
to –

JAMES. An' she's 'elped 'erself to 'is boots?

NELL. No.

JAMES. You been through 'is things?

NELL. No!

JAMES *goes to take hold of* NELL.

JAMES. Y'thieving –

GLADYS. She's not!

ADA. She didn't!

HANNAH. I did!

> JAMES *turns to* HANNAH. *Holds her gaze.*

> I got 'em and gave 'em to Nell. She's been playin' in work boots, 'er feet are… and she can't afford 'er own. Not yet, anyhow.

ADA. An' we're playing for soldiers.

JAMES. Soldiers.

GLADYS. To raise money for wounded soldiers. The New Zealand boys from the hospital… they came to watch us today and they thought it was –

JAMES. Amputees, are they?

GLADYS. Some are.

JAMES. Arms, legs, arms an' legs. Fingers shot off by their own hand to get 'em out the firing line.

GLADYS. We don't speak about it, we just –

NELL. Play.

JAMES. Maimed or blinded or out of 'is mind wi' shell shock while you're running around in 'is boots?

HANNAH. Now, it isn't her fault.

JAMES. The boots or the war?

NELL. She was just… Mrs Fairman, she was just being –

JAMES. What? (*To* HANNAH.) What were you being, ey?

HANNAH. A mother, that's all.

JAMES. Gals don't play football.

HANNAH. Father? They do.

15.

MAYA *is listening to* Grass in the Clouds.

IDA. You're listening to *Grass in the Clouds*, the go-to podcast for all things women's football.

SOPHIE. An' in this episode, we're looking back to look forward. Way back to women's football in World War One.

IDA. I know what you're thinking…

SOPHIE. A hundred years ago? No!

IDA. Well, buckle up cos This Is A Ride!

16.

Football pitch. From the static, a tap-tap of Morse code. Football commentator BRIAN BADEN *appears in a timeless sheepskin coat.*

BRIAN BADEN. When the cat's away, the mice will play. As the sons of England fight the Hun, their sisters and sweethearts man the factory and field. That's the sports field, Grandma. In Chelmsford and beyond, the fashion now is football – ladies' football – and, boy, these gals are game!

ADA, GLADYS, TRIXIE, NELL *and* MAUD *run out in Sterling Ladies blue-and-white-quartered kit. The five warm up before the game.*

Blue is the fetching colour of Sterling Telephone and Electrical Company's newborn side. The Dagenham girls join a growing army of workplace teams who play to raise funds for wounded men. Sterling made a stylish start to the season with a six–one stitch-up of City Shirtmakers, Burton Vowles. Keep a clean sheet in a four–nil whitewash of laundry girls, Brocks. The big guns came out for a four–nil annihilation of Vickers Dartford, smartly followed by a classy eight–two rout of Harrods, no less! Who says Victory is in the Kitchen? It's here, my dear, on the hallowed turf and in biblical rain, the mighty Blues are lining up for a gladiatorial showdown with unbeaten arch-rivals Marconi!

The players present themselves.

The sky's the limit for Sterling, their wireless sets found in spy planes. Will the pretty birds fly high today? We know the starting eleven. In goal, Miss Fairman, G. Outfield? Miss Fairman, A, her sister; Hale – Billet – Peters – Saggers – Mullett – Reader – Furlong – Foster – Marchant.

A referee's whistle. Sterling vs Marconi begins.

The Radio Girls have a season on Sterling. On a sodden pitch, it shows. A smooth slide tackle takes out Peters. Fairman A slipping and sliding. Reader dances around the puddles; Marchant struggles with pinpoint passing and oh, she's lost possession. Marconi on the break, closing in on goal, it's a one-to-one with Fairman G and oh! Sending out all the right signals, that's one–nil Marconi Ladies!

As a counterpoint, images of the Western Front may play. BRIAN BADEN *references key events and begins to take Sterling Ladies seriously.*

Marconi energised by their lead. Surging forward, fine attacking play. Sterling struggle to contain them. Both sides in a battle royal with the mud; the game plan abandoned, it's every girl for herself. Reader and Marchant soldier on; Fairman A chases every ball, Peters the midfield maestro but Marconi counter and off they go. Sterling run back, back, back, there must be ten players in the box, it's a goal-mouth scramble, Marchant clears but only as far as Fairman G – oh, she's dropped it and GOAL! Two–nil to Marconi! And with ten minutes to go, Sterling will have to dig deep to get any kind of a result from this. Billet on the ball now. To Saggers. Nice little one-two, she's up and away. Saggers to Hale to Foster. A lovely cross and it's Marchant now. Past one, two, three of the backline, she's in sight of goal and MARCHANT! Top-left the keeper stands no chance!

The fightback begins. No celebrations, they're back to the spot and bang, these girls mean business! Five minutes to go and the Blues surge forward with Fairman G holding the fort. Here's big sister now, looking dangerous. Reader unmarked but Fairman A wants to go it alone. Steaming into the six-yard box, the keeper dives, she shimmies left and ADA FAIRMAN, what a goal! She's levelled the game. Even Stevens, two–all.

Sterling celebrate the draw as if it's a victory. BRIAN's commentary accelerates through the spring of 1918.

Next, it's déjà vu all over again with a two–two draw with Vickers Combined. Sterling steams in with a titanic eleven–nil win over London General Omnibus Co. And who's that coming over the airwaves? It's the return of Radio Girls once again but they won't want this one broadcast: Marconi nil – Sterling five! What an astonishing season for Sterling Ladies, who've overthrown the Queens of Chelmsford to claim their crown. Highlights? Wins against Woolwich Arsenal (seven–one), Sopwith (three–nil) and Kynoch (three–nil). But don't just take my word for it. Everyone's talking.

ADA. The *Daily Mirror.*

TRIXIE. The *Tatler.*

MAUD. Pathé News.

GLADYS. The *New York Herald.*

ADA. 'Women are furnishing much of the athletic entertainment in Great Britain these war times.'

BRIAN BADEN. 'This group is the Sterling Ladies Football Club. The Unbeaten Women Champions of the Country.'

MAUD. Us?

ADA. Us.

NELL. The Dagenham Invincibles.

Flashbulb pops as they proudly pose for a team photo.

ACT TWO

1.

1918/2023. NELL *stands proud, a football in her hands, as* BRIAN BADEN *takes us through the opening four matches of Sterling's new season,* MAYA *watches Lauren James's England vs Nigeria crisis.*

BRIAN BADEN. September 1918. Season Two. Sterling Ladies strike up like a well-oiled machine with an eight–nil win against Docklands warehouse, Cairn Mills.

COMMENTARY (*voice-over*). Lauren James –

BRIAN BADEN. All aboard now for Kentish Town to dispatch Midland Rail eleven–nil.

COMMENTARY (*voice-over*). After all she's achieved in this tournament –

BRIAN BADEN. October sees the final Allied push towards the German border.

COMMENTARY (*voice-over*). What on earth was she thinking?

BRIAN BADEN. As the Central Powers begin to collapse, The Blues cruise to a fourteen–nil victory over W G Ducros.

COMMENTARY (*voice-over*). A moment of madness and frankly, I think it could be…

BRIAN BADEN. It's a goal-rush from the girls with none conceded by Fairman G in a riotous run of form.

COMMENTARY (*voice-over*). I think she'll be off.

BRIAN BADEN. All cylinders firing, the Dagenham dynamos play now with industrial strength; the workers become the machine.

COMMENTARY (*voice-over*). She is! Red card for stamping on the back of Alozie.

BRIAN BADEN. Who or what can beat them now?

COMMENTARY (*voice-over*). England's brightest light thus far, extinguished.

BRIAN BADEN. But just be sure you're ahead of the game, girls.

COMMENTARY (*voice-over*). What now for their World Cup campaign?

BRIAN BADEN. One slip and you're invincible no more.

2.

Maya's home. Monday August 7th 2023. 10.15 a.m. An anxious MAYA *watches England vs Nigeria on the big screen.*

COMMENTARY (*voice-over*). That's it. Full time. Penalties.

MAYA. Penalties…

COMMENTARY (*voice-over*). England battled on with ten players but now, it's spot-kicks to reach the quarter-finals.

MAYA. Dig deep, girls.

COMMENTARY (*voice-over*). England nil – Nigeria nil. For now.

MAYA. Dig deep…

SAMMY *comes home, dressed for work. The match volume drops.*

SAMMY. That went well.

I've only been sat in the 'ouse for an hour.

Sat like a lemon, three doors down.

Maya?

MAYA. What?

SAMMY. Accompanied viewing. Nine a.m. No-show.

MAYA. So?

SAMMY. 'So' what?

MAYA. You're at work whatever, you're still paid.

SAMMY. Ain't the point.

MAYA. If you say so.

SAMMY. It's rude. Disrespectful. An' it means I 'ave to go through me phone, check the comms, make sure I've done my job an' I'm not gonna land in the –

MAYA. Didn't you call 'em? The people.

SAMMY. Of course I did. Twice. Didn't pick up.

MAYA. Won't be you.

SAMMY. 'My time's more important than your time.'

MAYA. They'll be watching the match.

SAMMY *throws* MAYA *a look but she's fixed on the screen.*

SAMMY. You're right. Cos there's nothing else 'appening. Just this, that's all that matters.

MAYA. Lauren James got a red card.

SAMMY. Really?!

MAYA. She was marked out the game an' that's what it does to you, innit? Frustration. Ain't right but I get it.

SAMMY. An' then?

MAYA. We clung on. Now it's penalties.

SAMMY. At ten o'clock on a Monday morning…

MAYA. What else are you doing?

SAMMY. Working?!

MAYA. You can work for the rest of your life, Mum.

SAMMY. An' I will be at this rate. If you go to uni –

MAYA. 'A golden time, ain't it?'

SAMMY. Oh, so you do pay attention occasionally?

MAYA. 'Don't waste it. That's all I'm saying.'

    SAMMY *sees* MAYA *means it. The commentary rises.*

COMMENTARY (*voice-over*). England first. Georgia Stanway.

SAMMY. Oh, for God's sake…!

    SAMMY *relents and watches the match.*

COMMENTARY (*voice-over*). She's got the pedigree.

SAMMY. Let's hope.

COMMENTARY (*voice-over*). This for a quarter-final place.

SAMMY. An' I thought my job was stressful.

MAYA. Shut up.

COMMENTARY (*voice-over*). Georgia Stanway. (*Whistle.*) Oh, she misses the target altogether.

MAYA. No…

    MAYA *and* SAMMY *watch as a montage of penalties are played.*

COMMENTARY (*voice-over*). Mary Earps in the firing line. Can she hold her nerve?

SAMMY. Well, if anyone can…

MAYA. She's kept us in. Haiti, Denmark, without 'er…

COMMENTARY (*voice-over*). Oparanozie wide of the target!

MAYA. Wide!

COMMENTARY (*voice-over; whistle*). Beth England for England! She scores! – Michelle Alozie.

MAYA. Over!

COMMENTARY (*voice-over*). High as a kite!

MAYA. Yes!

COMMENTARY (*voice-over*). Daly.

MAYA. Wow!

COMMENTARY (*voice-over*). Goal! Two–nil England!

MAYA. Come on!

COMMENTARY (*voice-over*). Ajibade. Straight as an arrow!

SAMMY. Scores.

COMMENTARY (*voice-over*). Alex Greenwood.

MAYA. Yeeessss!

SAMMY. Well played.

COMMENTARY (*voice-over*). This is the high-stakes moment.

SAMMY. You don't say?

COMMENTARY (*voice-over*). If she fails to score here…

MAYA. Breathe…

COMMENTARY (*voice-over*). Ucheibe – Ice-cool!

SAMMY. Three–two?

MAYA. Three–two.

COMMENTARY (*voice-over*). Chloe Kelly.

SAMMY. Come on, gal.

MAYA. Match-winner.

COMMENTARY (*voice-over*). This to send them to the quarter-finals. (*Whistle*.)

MAYA. YES!!!!

COMMENTARY (*voice-over*). Kelly nails it! England go through!

MAYA. England!!!!

SAMMY. So, there you go.

COMMENTARY (*voice-over*). It's dark here but if you're watching at home this might go down as a daylight robbery. Nil–nil after a hundred and twenty minutes, England through to the quarter-finals on penalties.

MAYA. We were lucky, so lucky – on that performance – but Daly! Kelly!

SAMMY. The keeper! She's fearless, that gal.

MAYA. S'why Wiegman brought 'er back, innit?

SAMMY. Where from?

MAYA. She's part of the England squad, World Cup 2019. A year on, Neville drops 'er. She finds out on Instagram.

SAMMY. Jeez…

MAYA. She thinks it's all over but two years later, Sarina calls.

SAMMY. The Comeback Kid, ey?

MAYA. Wins the Euros an' then? The World Cup.

SAMMY. You think we can?

MAYA. I think we will.

MAYA *turns back to the TV.*

SAMMY. I was in a penalty shoot-out.

MAYA. Hockey?

SAMMY. Football.

MAYA. You what?!

SAMMY. I was ten, I think. A massive West Ham fan, we all were. I'd play outside with my brothers, on the common with the boys. Only girl but I loved it. Loved it. Then once, dunno why, one of the dads, he sets up this a little five-a-side tournament. The boys play for their street; if there ain't enough for a side where they live, they join the Wanderers. Who are strapped for a goalie an' ask yours truly.

MAYA. You never said.

SAMMY. A shoddy bunch but we got to the final. All-square at full time, it goes to pens. Sudden death. I dive the right way an' we win.

MAYA. Wow.

SAMMY. We get little medals, our photograph taken. An' that night, I say to your Nan… (*Thinks*.) Looking back, I dunno what I say but I remember the answer.

MAYA. Go on.

SAMMY. 'You're almost eleven. Come September, you go up to secondary school. An' the girls there don't…' That was that. I never played football again.

MAYA. Why didn't you tell us?

SAMMY. Cos it's a long time ago.

MAYA. Not that long.

SAMMY. An' it's silly. Stupid. Ridiculous, when you look at what they've done, what you've done, it's –

MAYA. It's what happened. To you an' the girls before you.

SAMMY. Thirty years back.

MAYA. A hundred years, Mum.

SAMMY. Whatever! So onwards an' upwards, ey? Right! (*Prepares to leave*.)

MAYA. I found this podcast –

SAMMY. To work –

MAYA. World War One? Up north, factory teams. They were playing to thousands of people on FA grounds till –

SAMMY. I ain't got time for an 'istory class.

MAYA. Women's football, I swear, it was big.

SAMMY. Not round 'ere.

MAYA. So big it was banned in the end.

SAMMY. Gotta go.

MAYA. Like you, in a way. Women have fought for a century, just for the right to –

SAMMY. Thank you, Germaine Greer.

MAYA. Who does she play for?

SAMMY. Google 'er.

    Exit SAMMY. MAYA *takes a moment to process what she's just heard.*

MAYA. Football… you played.

3.

Fairman home. A Saturday evening in October. NELL *cleans Ernest's boots with dubbin. She's meticulous in the work, giving them her undivided attention. At a certain point, she holds up the cleaning rag, as if it's imbued with magic. As she does,* JAMES *returns with a box of allotment potatoes and carrots.*

JAMES. What y'doing?

NELL. Nothin'.

    NELL *continues with her work.*

JAMES. What y'doing wi' them?

NELL. Dubbin.

JAMES. Dubbin?

    NELL *doubles down on the boots.*

NELL. Beeswax.

JAMES. I know what it is. Where d'you find it?

NELL. I bought it.

JAMES. You're s'posed to be saving for boots.

NELL. But these are me lucky ones now, so I wanna protect 'em. Wi' beeswax an' tallow an' oil.

JAMES. What's wrong wi' soap an' water.

NELL. Y'clean 'em with that but it dries 'em out, Cholly says.

JAMES. Well, if Cholly says –

NELL. Makes 'em stiff –

JAMES. Must be true –

NELL. Makes 'em crack. (*Beat.*) So y'soffen 'em wi' dubbin. Y'know, when you've just scored an 'at-trick in 'em…

JAMES. Only a three–nil win this time?

NELL. Nah. Fourteen.

JAMES. Potatoes, carrots an' beans. Give 'em a scrub when you're done.

JAMES puts the box down and turns to go.

NELL. Like the Royal Artillery, aren't we? Advancing.

JAMES. Are they?

NELL. 'Well, 'ere's to a time when the war is over an' we're all together again.'

Beat.

JAMES. You read 'is letters? Ernest?

NELL. With Ada. She's learning us, see.

JAMES watches as NELL returns to polishing her boots.

JAMES. You're doin' it wrong. You're not putting butter on bread. It's a thin film y'want.

NELL. 'Tis thin.

JAMES. Y'got 'alf the pot on the rag, come 'ere.

JAMES *takes the boot from* NELL.

NELL. We read stories, an' all. Fairy tales from the big book.

JAMES (*notices*). You've a stud loose.

NELL. *Red Riding 'ood. Cinderella. Aladdin.*

JAMES. Needs mending.

NELL. 'E finds a lamp an' when 'e rubs it like that –

JAMES. With a mucky old rag?

NELL. Out pops a genie who grants 'im three wishes.

JAMES. I know the story.

NELL. An' I know yours.

JAMES *returns to the stud, a distraction.*

JAMES. There's spares in a jam jar somewhere.

NELL. Yer wishes. Well, one of 'em. (*Nods to the boots.*) An'
'e will.

JAMES. You've a lot to say all of a sudden.

NELL. In't that sudden. We're into a new season.

JAMES. Don't I know it.

NELL. An' nearly all o' mine 'ave come true.

JAMES. Lucky you.

NELL. Learn to read. Ride a bike. Score twenty-six goals in
a real football team. Play on the Boleyn Ground, Upton Park.
'Ome of –

JAMES. You're playing West 'am?

NELL. LGOC. The Omnibus lot, Forest Gate. We walloped 'em
last year. The 'ammers, they 'eard 'of it. Set up a rematch on
their ground. Cholly says we'll get ten thousand in.

JAMES. On the Cabbage Patch.

NELL. No, the pitch.

JAMES. That's what we call it. Cos that's what it was 'fore they put up a stand. A field for potatoes an' cabbage.

NELL. So? Everyfing starts as som'fing.

JAMES. First match of the season, September 1911. Said to my boy 'You run out here one day.' Imagine that. A Fairman in claret an'…

NELL. Blue.

ADA *and* GLADYS *tumble in, both dressed for a dance and not expecting* JAMES *to be there.*

ADA. We now present to the Debutantes' Ball, Lady Ada Fairman of Park Lane –

GLADYS. Romford –

ADA. Accompanied by her chaperone for the season, the Dowager Lady Gladys –

Wrong-footed, ADA *and* GLADYS *come to a standstill. Their words cross.*

GLADYS. Father.

ADA. We didn't –

GLADYS. We thought you was at the –

ADA. Pub –

GLADYS. Allotment.

NELL. 'Ee weren't.

JAMES. What ball?

GLADYS. Oh, it's more of social –

ADA. Social evening.

GLADYS. Sports club.

ADA. Chess, draughts an' dancin'.

JAMES. Dancin'?

GLADYS. A little.

JAMES (*to* NELL). Y'going, an' all?

GLADYS. We've asked her.

NELL. Don't play draughts. Don't dance.

ADA. Cheer up, Cinders. She's left you a dress.

GLADYS. One of my castoffs that's better than most girls' best.

   JAMES *puts the boots down and retreats.*

ADA. An' y'don't 'ave to dance. If a gentleman asks, just say –

GLADYS. You're resting your feet from the match.

NELL. Some don't take no for an answer.

JAMES. So kick 'em where it 'urts.

NELL. An' I don't want the Spanish flu, ta very much.

ADA. But Nell, the 'ole team'll be there.

GLADYS. It won't be a night out wi'out you.

NELL. I can't, alright! I can't.

JAMES. Y'can and y'will.

NELL. Why should I?

JAMES. To give me an' their ma some peace, gal.

NELL. Alright!

JAMES. So get your glad rags on.

   ADA *raises an eyebrow to* GLADYS.

   Go!

   Exit NELL, ADA *and* GLADYS. JAMES *begins to repair* NELL*'s boot with a football stud from a jam jar of nails.*

4.

Fairman home. Later that night. Candlelight. JAMES *sits with the football boots. He picks one up. Runs his fingers over the leather. Studies its detail. Breathes the aroma of leather and dubbin. Puts a hand in. Holds it to his heart.*

In her own time and space, MAYA *listens to* Grass in the Clouds.

IDA. Then in 1915, the Football League's suspended and FA grounds fall silent. But in the factories, the women who stepped into the men's jobs are kicking a ball in the yard.

SOPHIE. Sport's seen as good for their health and don't laugh, their moral welfare.

IDA. Teams are formed and who knew? They're good. What starts as a bit of a spectacle moves into football league grounds.

SOPHIE. In the north-east of England, Blyth Spartans win the 1917 Munitionettes' Cup.

IDA. Same year, the mighty Dick, Kerr's Ladies are formed. With one of the greatest goal-scorers of British history – male or female – among 'em.

SOPHIE. Let's talk about Lily Parr.

In the flickering flame, HANNAH *returns.*

HANNAH. Penny?

JAMES. Huh?

HANNAH. Penny for your thoughts.

JAMES puts the boots down.

A ha'penny? A farthing?

JAMES. Y'just turn your mind, don't yer? To where 'e is… 'ow 'e is… what 'e's doin' while they're out dancin'.

HANNAH. Isn't that what he's fighting for, James?

JAMES. Who knows?

Beat.

HANNAH. Three years he's been lucky. Three years, Western Front –

JAMES. What's it done to 'im, ey? Will 'e even know us if he…

HANNAH. When 'e.

JAMES. What'll 'e be?

HANNAH. Our son. However – whatever – he is.

JAMES. An' our daughters?

HANNAH. They're safe an' well.

JAMES. Up 'ere? (*Taps his temple.*) With all they've been fed from…

HANNAH *picks her words.*

HANNAH. Alright… do we sit 'em down, tell 'em to stop?

JAMES. For what good it'll do.

HANNAH. You're the 'ead of the 'ouse, they'd 'ave to. I'd 'ave to.

JAMES. You've never done what you're told, woman.

HANNAH. That's why I married you, James.

Eye contact. A spark.

JAMES. A farm labourer. Widower. Four-year-old girl to raise.

HANNAH. A maid-of-all-work.

JAMES. All y'want's board an' lodgings.

HANNAH. But there you was – Prince Charming.

JAMES *almost smiles.*

JAMES. You do what you 'ave to in life.

HANNAH. Not just what you 'ave to, let's 'ope.

JAMES. Y'work to put food on the table an' shoes on their feet.

HANNAH. Learn 'em to walk.

JAMES. Show 'em the right path to walk down.

HANNAH. An' when it's time, let' em go.

JAMES. To fight for King and Country.

HANNAH. To play.

> *Beat.*

> We guide 'em, James. Then we support 'em.

> *Beat.*

> We should go.

JAMES. Go where?

HANNAH. To a match. Our girls' match. Upton Park.

JAMES. You?

HANNAH. They've been in the papers – Pathé News – seems everyone's seen 'em but us.

JAMES. You wanna go stand on a terrace? Go off ten miles to the Boleyn?

HANNAH. I won't lose me head for cheering 'em on.

JAMES. Cos you already 'ave.

HANNAH. I want to see 'em. An' I might catch a glimpse of myself at their age, who knows?

JAMES. Ey?

HANNAH. Not married wi' four kids to keep alive. Kicking an' running an' shooting an' scoring an'…

JAMES. Emancipated.

HANNAH. Free, James! Free. Before life takes back what it's given 'em.

JAMES. At least they've got a life.

HANNAH. For now.

A charged silence.

JAMES. Y'wanna go West Ham?

HANNAH. To see 'em, that's all.

JAMES. To call on Mrs Pankhurst.

HANNAH. Can I?

The question simmers.

Can we?

JAMES. We?

HANNAH. You took Ernest. Why can't you take me?

JAMES. Why d'you think?

HANNAH. He'd be going.

JAMES. It's not right, this.

HANNAH. If he could, he'd go in an 'eartbeat.

JAMES (*voice breaking*). It's not right.

HANNAH. What is any more, my love?

HANNAH *puts her hand on his.*

What is?

5.

Maya's home. Saturday August 12th. 12 45 p.m. MAYA *watches England vs Colombia. Her iPhone is close to hand.*

COMMENTARY (*voice-over*). We close in on half-time. In the knockout stages of the World Cup...

MAYA. We need a goal, come on!

COMMENTARY (*voice-over*). Usme, that's a good pass... and this might work out for Ospina... Caicedo... Santos... Santos, oh!!

MAYA. NO?!

COMMENTARY (*voice-over*). An absolutely brilliant goal from a brilliant player for Colombia.

MAYA. Shut up, it's a cross gone wrong!

COMMENTARY (*voice-over*). Is this another Colombian conquest in this World Cup?

MAYA *mutes the TV.*

MAYA. Shut up.

Agitated, she picks up her phone. Taps to play Grass in the Clouds. *Keeps her eyes fixed to the screen but listens to the podcast as it plays.*

SOPHIE. In 1918, the war ends but Parr and her Preston teammates play on, pulling crowds in the tens of thousands.

IDA. Gates only now – a century on – is women's football achieving again.

SOPHIE. So, what happened? In short, the FA.

IDA. December 1921: for reasons and excuses we'll interrogate, the wise men of the Football Association –

SOPHIE. 'Feel impelled to express their strong opinion that the game of football is quite unsuitable for females and ought not to be encouraged.'

IDA. 'The Council requests the clubs belonging to the Association refuse the use of their grounds for such matches.'

SOPHIE. A ban that remains for fifty years. Yes, you heard it right.

MAYA. Fifty…

MAYA *is distracted by the TV. She pauses the podcast and unmutes the TV sound.*

COMMENTARY (*voice-over*). Bronze wins the header. Might drop to Russo. Does. Not quite, oh!

MAYA. Get it!

COMMENTARY (*voice-over*). Spilt by the goalkeeper, she's made a right mess of it and England are level!

MAYA. Yeeeesss! Yeeeesss!

MAYA *reels around the house in celebration.*

6.

Sports ground. That night. Folk music plays and the football team partake in a folk dance. ADA *partners* TRIXIE, GLADYS *partners* NELL *and* MAUD *partners* CHOLLY. *The dance may be led by a* CALLER. *At a point where partners change,* GLADYS *finds herself with* CHOLLY. *Perhaps distracted, she turns on her ankle, shrieks and falls.*

CHOLLY. Gladys!

ADA. What y'doing?!

MAUD. Man down!

GLADYS. I'm fine, I just –

CHOLLY. Don't move.

GLADYS. Turned on my ankle, that's all.

NELL. Is it broke?

GLADYS. No!

ADA. It better not be.

NELL. You're the best goalie we got.

ADA. The only goalie.

NELL. Ain't forwards win matches, it's keepers.

TRIXIE. That's me told.

CHOLLY (*gesturing to her ankle*). May I?

GLADYS. It isn't – it won't –

> CHOLLY *lifts her foot, looks for tenderness, moves it to check the range of motion and locate the pain.*

CHOLLY. We'll see, how does that feel?

GLADYS. Fine. (*It isn't.*)

CHOLLY. If you move it like this…?

GLADYS. Alright… (*It really isn't.*)

CHOLLY. Could someone remove her shoe?

MAUD. Step back.

> MAUD *steps forward to remove* GLADYS*'s shoe.*

TRIXIE. It's like Cinderella backwards.

CHOLLY. Nell? Go get a cold compress.

NELL. A what?

ADA. A wet towel from the bar.

TRIXIE. An' a brandy.

GLADYS. I don't need a brandy.

TRIXIE. I do. If she's out –

GLADYS. Stop it! Stop talking like that, I'll be…

TRIXIE. You went down like a sack of spuds, Gladys.

ADA. I thought you'd got Spanish flu.

TRIXIE. Just like that?

ADA. That's what it does. You're fine one minute, the next you're gasping for breath, then you're gone.

TRIXIE. Flu? (*Laughing*.)

CHOLLY. Ain't broken.

MAUD. Could it be twisted?

CHOLLY. Let's hope not, that's four weeks out.

ADA. Never mind four weeks. 'Ow do we get 'er 'ome?

TRIXIE. Piggyback?

ADA. Three miles?

MAUD. Stretcher? Crutch?

ADA. Off a wounded soldier? Good luck wi' that.

CHOLLY. I'll walk her.

GLADYS. Y'don't have to.

CHOLLY. As gaffer, I do.

NELL. I'll come, an' all.

CHOLLY. No need.

NELL. To 'elp ya.

MAUD. We'll each take a leg an' an arm' –

GLADYS. You won't!

CHOLLY. An' what kind of signal does that send out? Bad news spreads like wildfire round 'ere.

TRIXIE. True enough.

CHOLLY. We're at full strength for Sat'day, right? Cos who are we?

NELL. The Invincibles.

CHOLLY. Who?

ALL. The Invincibles.

CHOLLY. You stay 'ere and dance until dawn.

> CHOLLY *offers* GLADYS *his arm and off she limps.*

ADA. Gaffer's orders.

> TRIXIE *puts out a hand to* ADA.

TRIXIE. May I have the pleasure…?

ADA. You're no gentleman.

TRIXIE. An' you're no lady, come 'ere!

> TRIXIE *pulls* ADA *into a hold and they dance away.*

MAUD. I 'ate dancing.

NELL. I 'ate it more. (*Takes a breath.*) You can't breathe with it, in 'ere.

> MAUD *pushes her to the door.*

MAUD. Come on, then. Out there!

7.

Maya's home. Half an hour later. MAYA *is hard-wired to the second half of England vs Colombia. As she watches,* SAMMY *comes in from work.*

COMMENTARY (*voice-over*). The one thing about this England side is even when they're not sparkling, they dig deep, they're gritty.

MAYA. They're closing you down, come on!

COMMENTARY (*voice-over*). They hang in there.

MAYA. Pick up the pace. Move the ball around.

COMMENTARY (*voice-over*). This is a side of winners.

SAMMY. Fight for it! Fight!

MAYA. What y'doing 'ere?

SAMMY. The match.

MAYA. If you wanna talk about clearing –

SAMMY. I don't. (*To the TV.*) Find the space!

MAYA. Are you drunk?

SAMMY *looks at* MAYA.

SAMMY. Find the space. That's what we've gotta…

COMMENTARY (*voice-over*). Here's Stanway.

MAYA*'s distracted by the commentary.*

SAMMY. Your results and their results –

MAYA. Through-ball.

SAMMY. Both of 'em –

MAYA. Arias, she's given it –

COMMENTARY (*voice-over*). Ooooh, Russo…?

SAMMY. Both matter. To you – and to me.

COMMENTARY (*voice-over*). Goal!!

SAMMY. Goal!

MAYA. WHAT A FINISH!

SAMMY. Woooooh!!

COMMENTARY (*voice-over*). Right on the money when England need her!

MAYA. Two–one!

COMMENTARY (*voice-over*). Cometh the hour, cometh Alessia Russo.

SAMMY. Two-freakin-one!

COMMENTARY (*voice-over*). Firing past Perez and England have turned this around.

SAMMY. An' that's what – Maya, look at me – the last two years, we'll turn it around. Cos what are we? What 'ave we always been?

MAYA. A team.

COMMENTARY (*voice-over*). This England side, when the chips are down, when you think they're beaten, when you think they're in trouble, they keep coming back.

SAMMY. There's nothing can beat us, remember? From day one, that's how it's been. You and me 'gainst the world.

MAYA. 'You' being the secret goalkeeping legend?

SAMMY. I was ten years old.

MAYA. So was Mary Earps, once upon a time. So was I.

SAMMY. That's different.

MAYA. Why? Tell us? (*Beat.*) Tell me your story.

8.

*Rural Dagenham. Later that night. Distant music from the
dance blends with the nocturnal sounds of the countryside.*
GLADYS *and* CHOLLY *are walking home;* TRIXIE *and* ADA
are outside the pavilion; NELL *and* MAUD *at the far end of the
field. A limping* GLADYS *needs to stop.*

GLADYS. I'm sorry.

CHOLLY. S'alright, take your time.

GLADYS. I'm sorry for…

CHOLLY. Perch 'ere a minute, come on. (*Guides her.*)

GLADYS. I'm sorry for being so stupid an' careless an' putting
the record at risk.

CHOLLY. Who says you 'ave?

GLADYS. We've Upton Park in a fortnight.

CHOLLY. Odds-on, you'll be fighting fit.

GLADYS. An' if I'm not?

CHOLLY. No one's indispensable, Gladys.

GLADYS. I ain't saying I am. (*Beat.*) Y'think I think I am?

CHOLLY. No.

GLADYS. It sounds like y'do.

CHOLLY. What I meant was –

GLADYS. 'It's gone to your 'ead.'

CHOLLY. No.

GLADYS. 'You think you're somebody special, now, ey?'

CHOLLY. Y'are.

GLADYS. An' I know I shouldn't be speakin' like this. You're
a man, you're management –

CHOLLY. What I'm trying to say is football ain't life an' death. (*Beat*.) Though sometimes, it feels… Let's get you to Park Lane. I'll come in, explain to your mother.

GLADYS. You don't 'ave to.

CHOLLY. From the movement you've got, I'd call it a sprain. Cold every couple of hours brings down the swelling; bandage it up; rest an' keep it raised. Walk on a stick if you have to.

GLADYS. Can I ride a bike?

CHOLLY. Do as you're told for a couple of weeks, you'll make it to Upton Park.

GLADYS. An' Handley Page?

CHOLLY. If I 'ave to, I'll put Maud Reader in goal.

GLADYS. Maud? She can't catch a cold.

CHOLLY. She plays cricket.

GLADYS. She clocks up the runs but fielding? All fingers an' thumbs.

CHOLLY. Well, that's not your worry, Miss Fairman. Come on. (*Offers an arm*.) 'Home, James, and don't spare the horses!'

GLADYS. I'm taking you of out your way, aren't I? If you live in Romford…

CHOLLY. I don't any more. I've a room on Osbourne Road.

GLADYS. Oh, nice.

CHOLLY. With an older couple. Retired schoolmaster, all very…

GLADYS. Quiet.

CHOLLY. A bit too quiet.

GLADYS. Sounds alright, it's bedlam at ours.

CHOLLY. They lost a grandson in June. Their second in six months.

GLADYS. Forgive me.

CHOLLY. For what?

GLADYS. It was clumsy –

CHOLLY. An' I try my best not to clatter around but I'm sure when they hear my key in the door, they're thinking… That's why it suits me. The football, the girls. Gets us out the house. Keeps us out.

GLADYS. It's good like that for us all.

CHOLLY. An' it's good to walk with you.

GLADYS. 'Obble.

CHOLLY. Talk to you. If it's not too forward to say.

GLADYS (*as* NELL). 'Ain't forwards win matches.'

CHOLLY. Keeper to keeper.

A frisson.

GLADYS. Go on, then. Talk.

Cross-fade to TRIXIE *and* ADA*, in the afterglow of hysterical laughter.* ADA *catches* TRIXIE*'s eye.*

ADA. Don't.

TRIXIE. What?

ADA. Don't do that.

TRIXIE. I ain't doin' nothin'.

ADA. Stop!

TRIXIE. What?!

ADA. Y'know very well.

TRIXIE. Y'looked at me, that's all.

ADA. You looked at me.

TRIXIE. Why would I?

ADA. We've come out –

TRIXIE. Before we were thrown out

ADA. To calm down, so do it.

TRIXIE. You just said don't do it.

ADA. STOP!

TRIXIE. Sssshuuush!

ADA. Sssshuuush!

Sound of a summer night.

TRIXIE. 'I thought you'd got Spanish flu.'

ADA. Ain't funny.

TRIXIE. So how come you're laughing?

ADA. Think of summin' else, quick.

TRIXIE. Like what?

ADA. Summin' sad, think!

TRIXIE puts on a sad face.

Sad… sad.

Cross-fade to NELL and MAUD, who is more attuned to the silence.

NELL. Quiet, innit?

MAUD. Still.

NELL. Still wha'? (*Beat.*) Joke.

MAUD. After twelve hours a day in the Machine Room, it's…

NELL. Don't you like work?

MAUD. Ain't that.

MAUD turns back to the sky.

NELL. What is it, then? What y'starin' at?

MAUD. I'm not staring. I'm gazing.

NELL. What cows do?

MAUD. That's grazing. I'm gazing into the great beyond. If that's what it is.

NELL *looks at the sky in a bid to see what* MAUD *sees*.

NELL. 'Tis big, I'll grant yer. The sky. Bigger 'ere than it looks up London.

MAUD. The moon's a silver shilling.

NELL. An' the silence. The silence out 'ere, it's…

MAUD. Deafening.

NELL. 'Tis.

MAUD. But the more y'listen, the more y'hear.

MAUD *nods to* NELL, *who tries to listen hard*.

NELL. Shells? Is it shells from the front y'can… Cos back 'ome, a woman told us y'could 'ear the Somme up on 'amstead 'eath.

MAUD *registers the thought*.

I've not never bin, so I don't know, but that's what she said.

MAUD. When I think of me brothers – all of 'em rogues – looking up at the same moon, it's…

NELL *looks up at the moon*.

NELL. My brother, 'e was a tailor's apprentice. The master'd flog 'im, I told 'im to go but 'e worked for 'is board an' lodgings – (*Beat.*) Then the dust o' the wool and the dyes, it got on 'is chest an'…

MAUD. How old was 'e?

NELL. Fourteen.

MAUD. I'm sorry to 'ear that, Nell.

NELL. Ta. But I'm one of eleven now, aren't I?

MAUD. I'm one of nine.

NELL. Football, I'm on about. Football. That's me family now.

MAUD. Me, an' all.

NELL. What does that make us, ey?

MAUD. Sisters.

As MAUD *looks at* NELL, *a kinship sparks. Cross-fade to* GLADYS *and* CHOLLY, *who are now engaged in a heart-to-heart.*

CHOLLY. Engineering and science, that's the future. In my view, anyway. Finding solutions from all we've learned from artillery, telegraphy… Industry working for peace and prosperity.

GLADYS. Imagine…

CHOLLY. We don't have to imagine. It's here, it's right in front of us. Sterling, Marconi, Hoffman's, Vickers… Methodical, rational, enquiring minds; ideas becoming reality; *changing* reality, irreversibly.

GLADYS. 'Ere's me thinking I just fuse one piece o'wire to another.

CHOLLY. You do. For air-to-ground transmission. Dashes and dots now but soon, very soon – the human voice. That's what's happening here an' now, Gladys. An' in my humble opinion, that's what they'll remember us for.

GLADYS. Who exactly?

CHOLLY. We're making history.

GLADYS. We're making a living, that's all.

CHOLLY. Oh ye of little faith.

GLADYS. Prospero's Farewell.

CHOLLY. *The Tempest.*

GLADYS. Y'know it?

CHOLLY. Do you?

GLADYS. A poor factory gal?

CHOLLY. That's not what –

GLADYS. We learned it at 'ome. Our father, he taught us by
  rote and we'd stand on the fireplace, reciting.

CHOLLY. Sadly, I played football at school not Shakespeare.

GLADYS. So, now's your chance, Mr Cholerton.

CHOLLY. Oh, I don't think so.

GLADYS. Why not?

CHOLLY. I'm no actor.

GLADYS. I dare ya.

> CHOLLY *takes the challenge and recites the piece to*
> GLADYS. *At first, she prompts him but they soon fall into*
> *step with one another.*

CHOLLY.
  Our revels now are ended. These our actors,
  As I foretold you, were all spirits, and
  Are melted into air…

GLADYS.
  Into thin air.

CHOLLY.
  And like the baseless fabric of this vision,
  The cloud-capp'd towers –

GLADYS.
  The gorgeous palaces –

CHOLLY.
  The solemn temples –

GLADYS.
  The great globe itself –

CHOLLY.
  Yea, all which it inherit, shall dissolve,
  And like this insubstantial pageant faded,
  Leave not a rack behind.

GLADYS *spins around and releases a call to the heavens.*

GLADYS.
We are such stuff as dreams are made on!

CHOLLY. You surely are.

GLADYS *turns back to* CHOLLY.

GLADYS.
And our little life is rounded – ooops!

GLADYS *stumbles on her ankle.* CHOLLY *catches her.*

CHOLLY. Gotcha.

Eyes meet.

GLADYS. With a kiss.

CHOLLY. Ain't it 'sleep'?

GLADYS *kisses* CHOLLY.

GLADYS. Not tonight.

CHOLLY *returns the kiss. Cross-fade to* TRIXIE *and* ADA, *thinking.*

ADA. Well?

TRIXIE. I've got brain-ache.

ADA. I've thought of summink.

TRIXIE. Work on Monday.

ADA. What happens when it's over. (*Not a question.*)

TRIXIE. The weekend?

ADA. The season. Come April.

TRIXIE. Six months yet. We got two games a month before –

ADA. Marconi 'ave packed up already. Kynoch's an' Vickers, they're laying girls off now the war's…

TRIXIE. Ain't over yet.

ADA. But they are coming 'ome. Who are we playing for then?

TRIXIE. There'll still be wounded soldiers.

ADA. Don't sound so glad about it.

TRIXIE. I'm not. Course I'm not. All I'm saying is –

ADA. What 'appens when Ernest –

TRIXIE. We don't need a reason to play –

ADA. When 'e's back for the rest of 'is –

TRIXIE. We're the Invincibles. We *are* the reason.

    Beat.

ADA. Only takes one letter.

TRIXIE. To him?

ADA. The name. To make us invisible.

TRIXIE. What y'on about now?

ADA. Invincible. Lose the 'n' an' we're nowhere.

    TRIXIE *considers the thought.*

TRIXIE. Invisible's spelt with an 's' innit?

ADA. Y'know what I'm saying.

TRIXIE. It's two letters.

ADA. So?

TRIXIE. Y'donkey.

ADA. You're a donkey.

TRIXIE. An' I'll always see ya. (*Beat.*) Always.

    The night hums around them.

ADA. You still write to 'im, don't'cha?

TRIXIE. Every week.

ADA. Do you tell him about it?

TRIXIE. Some of it.

ADA. What of it?

TRIXIE. The raising money, the 'keeping yer spirits up' bit.

ADA. An' 'e writes back?

TRIXIE. When 'e can.

ADA. Does 'e say things about it? The future.

TRIXIE. It's all 'e says.

ADA. Oh?

TRIXIE. Cos they 'ave to 'old on to it, don't they?

ADA. Coming 'ome. Back to work. (*Beat*.) Wedding plans.

TRIXIE. All that.

   Beat.

ADA. Will you still play when you're married?

TRIXIE. One step at a time, ey?

ADA. Do you think he'll let ya?

TRIXIE. Ah, you know Ernest.

ADA. What if 'e's changed?

TRIXIE. We've all changed. Nothing's the same no more, is it?

ADA. No.

TRIXIE. So we've just gotta…

ADA. Wait an' see.

TRIXIE (*sings*).
   When Tommy comes marching home again…

ADA. Father's favourite.

TRIXIE. With 'is sparkly eyes an' 'is scarecrow 'air.

ADA. Too pretty by 'alf for a soldier-boy.

TRIXIE. Weren't they all, though? Looking back.

ADA. God 'elp us if 'e don't come home.

A metaphorical chill in the air.

TRIXIE. We're supposed to be out for a knees-up?

ADA. We was.

TRIXIE. Till your sister fell flat on 'er face.

ADA. That is what y'call a good night.

TRIXIE. A good time. That's what we're 'aving, innit?

ADA. A wonderful time. An' I don't want it ever to end.

TRIXIE. I know.

ADA. What would you rather be, Trixie? Me sister-in-law or me teammate?

TRIXIE. Ain't a choice.

ADA. If it was?

TRIXIE looks at ADA. *Knows the answer. Can't say it out loud.*

TRIXIE. Ain't tonight.

TRIXIE throws an arm around ADA. *Pulls her towards her. Pretends to throttle her.*

ADA. Don't do that?!

TRIXIE. What?

ADA. That!

TRIXIE. Cos I can! Cos I can.

TRIXIE and ADA *play like puppies. Cross-fade to* NELL *and* MAUD, *whose conversation is starting to flow.*

MAUD. I've three sisters – five brothers – not one of 'em got on wi' Dad. I went to live at the pub at sixteen to cook an' clean for me gran.

NELL. An' sling out a few o' the drunkards.

MAUD. Oh, she didn't need no 'elp wi' that.

NELL. She gone now?

MAUD. But I'm still there wi' me aunt an' uncle. A room to meself. Up in the eaves like a bat.

NELL. What I wouldn't give for that.

MAUD. Back 'ome?

NELL. Ain't going 'ome.

MAUD. No?

NELL. No. (*Beat.*) I'm gonna stop 'ere at the Sterling.

MAUD. An' the Fairmans?

NELL. Not in a bed wi' Gladys. She kicks like she does on the park.

MAUD. Kick 'er back.

NELL. They'd kick me out.

MAUD. We got paying guests at the pub. If a room comes up, I can put in a word wi' me aunt.

NELL. Would ya?

MAUD. Why wouldn't I?

The night hums around them.

NELL. I'm gonna live 'ere for the rest of me life.

MAUD. S'pose I will, an' all.

NELL. An' I tell yer, I'll fly on the wing till I'm forty.

MAUD. Y'mean that?

NELL. No, fifty.

MAUD. Y'don't think it makes yer what some of 'em say? (*Beat.*) 'A man on the inside', all that.

NELL. Do you think we are?

MAUD *considers the question.*

MAUD. I'm not a man when I'm playing.

NELL. I'm not a gal.

MAUD. No?

NELL *thinks of what it is and how she feels when she's playing.*

NELL. I'm a spark, a flame, a fire.

MAUD. The sun an' the moon an' the sky.

NELL. I'm alive. I'm me. I'm free.

9.

Football pitch. November 1918. White noise, Morse code and BRIAN BADEN*'s commentary.*

BRIAN. Do strikers or keepers win games? We're about to find out. As Sterling line up against Handley Page, the stakes have never been higher. With Fairman G out with an ankle sprain, can Reader keep a clean sheet? Well, the answer is yes as the Blues rinse their oppo by four goals to nil. Only four, you ask? Well, November's Spanish flu epidemic is taking its toll on fitness and fixtures combined. The November clashes with Sopwith and Gnome are cancelled due to the rising threat and... oh, what's this?

NELL *stops playing. She is fighting for breath. She brings the game to a standstill.*

Marchant looks like she's struggling here. She's breathing hard. Too hard. The girls come to her aid, the referee calls for assistance... Sterling could be in trouble here. Oh dear... I don't like the look of this one little bit.

NELL *falls to her knees, gasping for breath. All the team come to her aid. As* NELL *gasps for breath, a trumpeter plays 'The Last Post'.*

10.

Churchyard. November 1918. The pitch now hosts the grieving team, JAMES *and* HANNAH, *and* CHOLLY. *All sing 'Abide with Me'.*

ALL.
Abide with me; fast falls the eventide
The darkness deepens; Lord with me abide
When other helpers fail and comforts flee
Help of the helpless, O, abide with me.

I fear no foe with Thee at hand to bless;
Ills have no weight and tears no bitterness
Where is death's sting? Where, grave, thy victory?
I triumph still if Thou abide with me.

The hymn draws to a close but the team remain as the sun begins to set.

TRIXIE. The Invincibles.

GLADYS. It's a word, that's all.

ADA. A lie.

TRIXIE. We've lost 'er.

GLADYS. Our winger.

MAUD. Our sister.

TRIXIE. Our friend.

MAUD. Our team.

GLADYS. Our game.

Silence.

ADA. Retribution, isn't it?

HANNAH. What for?

ADA. Laughing an' joking. Running an' jumping an' dancing when people are dying. Putting on men's clothes an' acting like inverts.

CHOLLY. Who calls you that?

ADA. They don't 'ave to. You see it, you feel it. 'Girls don't play football.' (*Glancing at her father.*) They're right.

HANNAH. This is nothing to do with –

ADA. It's our comeuppance

HANNAH. Nell was fragile, she 'ad a weak chest –

TRIXIE. An' a lion heart.

HANNAH. You're a pride of lions.

GLADYS. Not now.

ADA. No more.

Silence.

CHOLLY. The night's drawing in.

HANNAH. Should we…? (*Gestures to go.*)

CHOLLY. I think so, don't you?

MAUD. A spark – a flame – a fire. A torch we'll carry to Upton Park.

TRIXIE. How?

GLADYS. No.

ADA. We can't.

JAMES. You can an' you will. Cos to see a Fairman run out at the Boleyn…

JAMES *takes* HANNAH*'s hand and turns to his daughters.*

You'll play, d'you hear me? You'll play.

11.

Maya's home. Wednesday August 16th. MAYA watches England vs Australia. The match holds her in a poetic soundscape. NELL is watching with her.

COMMENTARY (*voice-over*). England v Australia –
World Cup Semi-Final –
It's Toone!
Yes! Ella Toone!
What a scorcher!
One–nil England!
Russo.
Dispossessed.
Sam Kerr.
Oh!!! What about that!
The Matilda's brightest star –
England with a battle to fight.
Hemp! That's two! Back in the game!

MAYA *becomes aware* NELL *is watching, listening and feeling every moment.*

The seconds pass –
Five minutes and counting –
England under pressure –
Wonderful run from Hemp –
Still she runs –
She flies –

NELL. A spark.

MAYA. A flame.

NELL *and* MAYA. A fire.

COMMENTARY (*voice-over*). Beautiful ball!
Russoooo!

'RUSSOOOO' bleeds into BRIAN BADEN*'s commentary.* MAYA *and* NELL *celebrate the goal together.*

BRIAN BADEN. Anne Boleyn may have lost her head but Sterling Ladies keep theirs, executing a five–nil defeat of LGOC at Upton Park.

COMMENTARY (*voice-over*). Majestic!

MAYA. Russoooo!

BRIAN BADEN. We hear the echo of Tilbury…

NELL. 'I know I have the body of a weak and feeble woman!'

MAYA. 'But I have the heart and stomach of a king!'

BRIAN BADEN. And the Queens of English football?

COMMENTARY (*voice-over*). England on course for the World Cup Final!

BRIAN BADEN. Undefeated!

12.

Sports ground. November 11th, 1918. From the England vs Australia celebrations comes Morse code, tapping out news of the Armistice. A rumour swiftly spreads. Workers are called to assemble. Church bells strike eleven o'clock. BURNEY mounts a podium.

BURNEY. At ten twenty a.m., the Prime Minister, David Lloyd George, announced the Armistice was signed at five o'clock this morning. Hostilities are to cease on all fronts from eleven a.m. today. The Allied terms are accepted: the disarmament and demobilisation of all German forces begins. The Kaiser has abdicated and the last guns are fired on the Home Front. Our brave men and women on battlefield, factory and workshop: Victory is won.

ALL. Hoorah-hoorah!

Flags are unfurled. Cheers follow and punctuate the speech. GLADYS, ADA, TRIXIE and MAUD will find one another other as the speech unfolds. A rising chorus of 'Land of Hope and Glory' is sung as lustily as on the terraces. Patriotic singing, flags, decorations may blend with World

*Cup celebrations. 'Land of Hope and Glory' becomes
a football chant.*

We 'ate Woolwich Arsenal
We 'ate Marconi too (and Hoffman's!)
We 'ate Dartford Vickers
But Sterling, we love you!

Amidst the exuberance, GLADYS *sees* CHOLLY *is alone.
She approaches with a little uncertainty. As she does,* ADA
finds TRIXIE.

ADA. It's over.

TRIXIE. It is.

ADA. They're coming 'ome.

TRIXIE. They are.

ADA. 'E is.

TRIXIE. 'E is.

As the celebrations flow around them, TRIXIE *throws her
arms around* ADA *and holds her as tight as she can.*

CHOLLY. Forgive me.

GLADYS. For?

CHOLLY. Not sweeping you up in a victory… (*Gestures to the
dancing.*)

GLADYS. Oh, y'know me an' dancin'.

CHOLLY. I wish I was that kind of man but …

GLADYS. It was a one-off.

CHOLLY. Gladys, I don't mean… it wasn't, it isn't… oh…

GLADYS. Something we need to discuss? I know.

CHOLLY. But I took advantage.

GLADYS. Actually, I think I took advantage of you. Being
twenty-three years old with a war on, an' thinking I might
die without knowing – y'know – what a kiss was.

CHOLLY. It was more than a kiss.

GLADYS. Not much more.

CHOLLY. Thankfully.

GLADYS. Really?

CHOLLY. I don't mean you weren't… you are, of course you are and if you were older… oh, I'm really no good at this.

GLADYS. You're not. But if you was, you wouldn't be you.

GLADYS *kisses* CHOLLY.

CHOLLY. Careful.

GLADYS. Nobody cares, Cholly. Not today. An' as you say, if we're careful…

CHOLLY. When?

GLADYS. No time like the present.

CHOLLY. Gladys…

GLADYS. Oh, come on. What's the worst that can happen?

CHOLLY. A shotgun wedding?

GLADYS. I'll deal wi' me father. You deal wi' me.

GLADYS *kisses* CHOLLY *in full view.*

CHOLLY. Armistice Day.

GLADYS. Ain't it?

As the celebrations reach a crescendo, GLADYS *and* CHOLLY *disappear.*

13.

Maya's home. August 19th, 10.55 a.m. MAYA *watches the World Cup Final pre-match atmosphere as* SAMMY *bustles in.*

SAMMY. 'Ave I missed it?

MAYA. What y'doing?

SAMMY. The National Anthem –

MAYA. Upstairs –

SAMMY. So-called.

MAYA. Banging about.

SAMMY. 'God Save the King', ain't the same.

MAYA. It's nearly kick-off.

SAMMY. I know! (*Beat.*) I know.

   SAMMY *presents an old, small, circular stud to* MAYA.

MAYA. What's this?

SAMMY. A lucky charm but careful, it's sharp.

   MAYA *looks at the item: a small round oxidised barrel with three pins.*

MAYA. Where's it from?

SAMMY. You'll never guess? Yesterday, three doors down –

MAYA. Cut to the chase.

SAMMY. I spy this display on a shelf. Old curiosities found by the vendor under the floor when he rips out the kitchen.

MAYA. Mum, I don't care.

SAMMY. Then I recall something left in our loft.

MAYA. Later.

SAMMY. A jam jar. Full of old nails an' such.

MAYA. It's the World Cup Final –

SAMMY. So up I go. Dig it out. An' I'm right, there's more of 'em there.

MAYA. Drawing pins.

SAMMY. Studs, he says. Football studs.

MAYA *takes another look.*

MAYA. Off an old pair of boots?

SAMMY. From the days they nailed 'em in.

MAYA (*taps the pins on her hand*). Nah…

SAMMY. He's researched it, he knows 'is stuff.

MAYA. Three little spikes in a barrel?

SAMMY. Could be a hundred years old.

MAYA. Okay… (*Turns it around in her fingers.*)

SAMMY. Funny, innit? What's left behind; what survives.

MAYA. Funny they're in both the 'ouses.

SAMMY. Lads who played together, who knows?

MAYA. Or girls?

SAMMY. Or girls.

MAYA. Yeh…

SAMMY. So, go on, make a wish on it.

MAYA (*amused*). No!

SAMMY. Fine!

SAMMY *takes the stud and holds it tight.*

I wish two–nil England. No extra time, no penalties.

MAYA. Three–nil, Lauren James hat-trick.

SAMMY. She's on the bench.

MAYA. A wish, you said, not a prediction.

SAMMY. Go on, push your luck.

SAMMY *offers* MAYA *the stud. She takes it. Closes her fist around it.*

MAYA. I'll make a promise instead?

SAMMY. That's allowed.

An energy; a ripple in time.

MAYA. To take this gap year an' fill it with football.

SAMMY. Three Bs? You can do whatever you like.

MAYA. To get fit. Match-fit. To play again. Home team, grassroots an' deeper, y'know? For the women whose stories were buried; the girls who were shamed; for all those lost, forgotten teams and for you, Mum, who never had one. Yeh... I'll play for the love of the game.

SAMMY. Ain't just a game. It's what you are, gal. Who you are.

MAYA. An' it's just the beginning.

From the pre-match atmosphere, the countdown: ten, nine, eight, seven, six, five...

SAMMY. My God, it is!

MAYA. England. World Cup Final.

SAMMY. If the ten-year-old me knew this day was coming...

MAYA. She'd still be playing.

SAMMY. With the veterans.

MAYA. Why not? Walking football? A toe in the water...?

SAMMY. Who knows, ey?!

COMMENTARY (*voice-over*). Here we go, underway, Down Under for the final time. England did it at home, can they do it in Sydney?

MAYA. Yes!

SAMMY. Bring it home, England!

MAYA. BRING IT HOME!

14.

Sports field. A Saturday in April. 1919. Twilight. The World Cup Final atmosphere bleeds into BRIAN BADEN*'s round-up of Sterling Ladies' final games. The company sing 'In Flanders Fields' by John McCrae.*

COMPANY.
In Flanders fields, the poppies blow
Between the crosses, row on row,
That mark our place: and in the sky
The larks, still bravely singing, fly.

BRIAN BADEN. And what a remarkable season it's been. November 16th: Sterling Ladies pick themselves up and return to the fray with a ten–nil win against AEC Walthamstow. Victories over GE Railway Stores, Woolwich Arsenal and RAF Sutton Men. Handley Page return for a six–nil drubbing this time and Sterling's run ends on April 26th 1919 with a two–nil win over Hoffman's of Chelmsford in front of four thousand spectators.

As BRIAN *is recounting their glories,* ADA, GLADYS, TRIXIE *and* MAUD *appear on the field of play in mud-stained, maybe even bloodstained kit. We see every tackle and every fall. As soldiers returning from the battlefield, each has a medal on her chest.*

COMPANY.
Scarce heard amid the guns below,
We are the Dead. Short days ago
We lived, felt dawn, saw sunset glow
Loved and were loved, and now we lie
In Flanders fields.

BRIAN BADEN. The stats? Over two years, Sterling Ladies play thirty-six, win thirty-four, draw two and lose none. They score two hundred and one goals, concede fourteen and remain unbeaten. Will we ever see their like again?

BRIAN *is momentarily lost for words. He takes a moment.*

'Mother, what did you do in the war?' When little Johnny asks, these women will tell him: 'We played a beautiful game.'

ADA. Beautiful?

GLADYS. We were fighters.

TRIXIE. Every step of the way.

MAUD. Got the medals to prove it.

GLADYS. 'Presented by the Sterling Telephone and Electrical
Company to the Sterling Ladies Football Club. President
Guy Burney Esquire. Undefeated.

ADA. We put Nell's in a box wi' the newspaper cuttings.

GLADYS. Cos someone might come for 'em someday.

Beat.

MAUD. I see her everywhere, don't you?

ADA. Forever blue.

TRIXIE. Aren't we all?

ADA. We'll see.

TRIXIE. War work's finished. Marconi, Vickers, Hoffmann's,
the Omnibus lot? The jobs are gone, the girls are gone.
There's no one to play.

MAUD. Not round 'ere, anyhow.

TRIXIE. It's over an' done.

ADA. Perhaps not forever?

TRIXIE. Forever? I want it now.

TRIXIE *pulls off her shirt and throws it down.*

ADA. What y'doing?

TRIXIE. Taking up drinkin' an' smokin' an' swearin'. An'
putting a brick through the window of them who've took this
away from us.

GLADYS. No one's took nothing.

TRIXIE. They gave it, they took it an' what are we left with?

ADA. Peace.

TRIXIE. Not in 'ere. (*Hand to chest*). Cos it already feels like it 'appened to somebody else. Somebody better an' stronger than me.

ADA. You're a footballer, Trixie.

GLADYS. You'll always be a –

TRIXIE. Fool. For thinking it's something we'd always be able to…

ADA. Do.

GLADYS. Have.

MAUD. Be.

TRIXIE. Still… So what? Life goes on. S'only a game, innit?

Maybe the tap of Morse code? And from another time and place, the echo of 2023 World Cup commentary.

COMMENTARY (*voice-over*). And it's over. Broken hearts for England.

TRIXIE turns to go. ADA calls after her.

ADA. Trixie Peters.

Gladys Fairman.

Maud Reader.

GLADYS and MAUD catch on to what ADA is saying.

GLADYS. Ada Fairman.

MAUD. Alice Saggers.

ADA. Maud Billet.

GLADYS. Edie Mullet.

MAUD. Vera Hale.

ADA. May Furlong.

GLADYS. Violet Foster.

TRIXIE turns back.

TRIXIE. Nell Marchant.

MAUD. Sterling Ladies. Unbeaten.

An echo of World Cup commentary. 'In Flanders Fields' is sung.

COMMENTARY (*voice-over*). Beaten by the better team on the night, the Lionesses will roar again but it wasn't meant to be.

COMPANY.
Take up our quarrel with the foe;
To you from failing hands we throw
The torch; be yours to hold it high.
If ye break faith with us who die
We shall not sleep, though poppies grow
In Flanders fields.

TRIXIE. Why us? I mean looking back… how did we do it?

ADA. We worked 'ard.

MAUD. Trained 'ard.

GLADYS. Played 'ard.

MAUD. But why us? What did we 'ave that no one else…

GLADYS. Cholly?

ADA. Aye-aye.

MAUD. Nell.

GLADYS. An' whatever it takes to win.

TRIXIE. Win what, though? In the end?

The light is fading as the question hangs in the air.

COMMENTARY (*voice-over*). Full-time in the 2023 World Cup Final. Spain one – England nil.

MAUD. Shall we let history settle that?

TRIXIE. History, us?

MAUD. Why not? One day.

ADA. When there's a Romford Ladies, a West Ham Ladies –

MAUD. An England Ladies, who knows?

TRIXIE. In your dreams.

GLADYS. 'We are such stuff as dreams are made on.'

ADA. Veni, vidi, vici.

TRIXIE. I came, I saw, I conquered.

The four women stand in defiance of the setting sun. A final World Cup commentary.

COMMENTARY (*voice-over*). In 1921, the FA declared football was 'quite unsuitable for females'. A century on, we know the score: the 2023 World Cup is a triumph for equality, courage and justice; a victory for all those who fought – and keep on fighting – to play.

ALL. The Invincibles.

The End.

www.nickhernbooks.co.uk

 facebook.com/nickhernbooks

 twitter.com/nickhernbooks